United States of America: A Safe Haven for Torturers

Amnesty International has issued a series of publications as ⌐ of its worldwide Campaign to Stop Torture, which w⌐⌐ ' October 2000:

- *Take a Step to Stamp Out Tortur*
- *Hidden Scandal, Secret Shame—1 of Children* (AI Index: ACT 40/038/20⌐
- *Broken Bodies, Shattered Minds—To* ⌐⌐ *reatment of Women* (AI Index: ACT 40/001/2001);
- *Stopping the Torture Trade* (AI Index: ACT 40/002/2001);
- *Crimes of Hate, Conspiracy of Silence: Torture and Ill-Treatment Based on Sexual Identity* (AI Index: ACT 40/016/2001);
- *Racism and the Administration of Justice* (AI Index: ACT 40/020/2001);
- *End Impunity—Justice for the Victims of Torture* (AI Index: ACT 40/024/2001).

The campaign aims to galvanize people around the world to join the struggle to end torture.

- Join Amnesty International USA and other organizations that fight torture.
- Make a donation to support Amnesty International's work.
- Take action online at www.amnestyusa.org/stoptorture/. Visitors to the website will be able to appeal on behalf of individuals at risk of torture.

Cover: Retired Peruvian army major Tomás Ricardo Anderson Kohatsu, who is accused of torture, at Ronald Reagan National Airport in Washington, DC, on March 9, 2000. Anderson Kohatsu was questioned by the Justice Department later that day in Houston, Texas, but was allowed to return to Peru after the State Department intervened and asserted that Anderson Kohatsu was entitled to diplomatic immunity.
AFP Photo

Amnesty International is a worldwide human rights activist movement with more than 1.1 million members in over 140 countries and territories, including nearly 300,000 members in the United States.

Amnesty International's vision is of a world in which every person enjoys all of the human rights enshrined in the Universal Declaration of Human Rights and other international human rights standards.

Amnesty International undertakes research and action focused on preventing and ending grave abuses of the rights to physical and mental integrity, freedom of conscience and expression, and freedom from discrimination, within the context of its work to promote all human rights.

Amnesty International is independent of any government, political ideology, or religious creed. It does not support or oppose any government or political system. It is concerned solely with the impartial protection of human rights.

Amnesty International is funded largely by its worldwide membership and by donations from the public.

United States of America:
A Safe Haven for Torturers

Amnesty International USA Publications

The principal author of this report is William J. Aceves.

First published in 2002 by
Amnesty International USA
322 Eighth Avenue
New York, NY 10001

www.amnestyusa.org

© Copyright
Amnesty International USA Publications 2002
ISBN: 1-887204-32-6
Original language: English

Printed by:
Globe Litho
One Teaneck Road
Ridgefield, NJ 07660

CONTENTS

The research for this Report was conducted prior to the September 11, 2001 attacks that caused the injury and death of thousands of people in the United States. Amnesty International expresses its deepest sympathy for the victims and their families and calls for those responsible for these crimes against humanity to be brought to justice, in full accordance with international human rights and humanitarian law.

But in seeking justice, governments should remain vigilant about respecting human rights. Indeed, it is in times of crisis that human rights, particularly those of vulnerable groups such as immigrants and refugees, are most threatened. Amnesty International therefore urges the U.S. Government to ensure that any measures taken in the pursuit of justice are implemented in ways that do not undermine fundamental protections. Respect for human rights and due process should always guide efforts to combat impunity so that the search for justice is not undermined.

The purpose of this Report, which is being issued in connection with Amnesty International's Campaign to Stop Torture, is to outline measures that the U.S. Government should take to ensure that it is not a safe haven for perpetrators of torture and other grave human rights abuses. Nothing in this Report should, however, be construed as a justification for making it more difficult for legitimate immigrants and refugees to enter and remain in the United States. Nor should anything in this Report be construed as a justification for suspending due process or violating the right of all human beings to be protected from torture or other cruel, inhuman or degrading treatment. The United States has benefited greatly from allowing immigrants to enter the country and has a responsibility under national and international law to protect individuals fleeing war and persecution.

1: Preface

"It's not [about] collecting money, it's about collecting justice. Justice for all."
—Edgegayehu Taye[1]
Torture survivor from Ethiopia who sued
one of the alleged perpetrators in a U.S. court

In 1993, the U.S. District Court for the Northern District of Georgia made the following findings of fact in a civil action filed by Ethiopian torture victims against Kelbessa Negewo, a former Ethiopian government official.

> On January 6, 1978, plaintiff Abebe-Jiri was arrested again along with her 16-year-old sister Yesharge. She was taken to the same prison. At the prison in Şubzone 10, she was interrogated and tortured in the presence of defendant Negewo and several other men for a period of several hours. She was told to take off her clothes. Her arms and legs were then bound, and she was whipped with a wire on her legs and her back. She suffered severe pain. She was repeatedly threatened with death if she did not reveal the location of a gun. At all times, the interrogation and torture of plaintiff Abebe-Jiri was conducted in a humiliating and degrading manner.
>
> Defendant Negewo personally supervised at least some part of the interrogation and torture of plaintiff Abebe-Jiri. He also personally interrogated her and participated directly in some of the acts of torture of plaintiff Abebe-Jiri.[2]

Based upon these findings, the District Court concluded that Kelbessa Negewo had committed acts of torture and other cruel, inhuman or degrading treatment. As a result, the Court awarded

---

1 CNN Morning News, March 31, 1998. See *infra* Section 5.

2 *Abebe-Jiri v. Negewo*, No. 1:90-CV-2010-GET, 1993 WL 814304 (N.D.Ga. Aug. 20, 1993) *aff'd* 72 F.3d 844 (1996).

the plaintiffs compensatory and punitive damages in the amount of $1.5 million, which has not been collected.

The Immigration and Naturalization Service ("INS") was purportedly notified of the District Court's ruling. Notwithstanding, the INS approved Negewo's pending application for naturalization and granted him U.S. citizenship.[3] Mr. Negewo remains a U.S. citizen and currently resides in the United States.

The case of Kelbessa Negewo is not unique. All too often, individuals who have committed torture or other human rights abuses in other countries have been allowed to enter and reside in the United States with impunity, in some cases even settling in the same communities as their victims.

---

[3] *See How a Torture Figure Becomes a Victim,* FULTON COUNTY DAILY REPORT, March 2, 1998.

2: Introduction

"Torture is prohibited by law throughout the United States. It is categorically denounced as a matter of policy and as a tool of state authority. Every act constituting torture under the Convention [against Torture] constitutes a criminal offense under the law of the United States. . . . The United States is committed to the full and effective implementation of its obligations under the Convention [against Torture] throughout its territory."
—U.S. Department of State[4]
Initial Report to the U.N. Committee against Torture

It would undoubtedly surprise most Americans to learn that perpetrators of human rights abuses from around the world live in the United States.[5] In the past year alone, the Immigration and Naturalization Service ("INS") has identified numerous individuals in the United States who allegedly committed human rights abuses abroad.[6] Some of these individuals have been deported.[7] Other individuals identified by the INS remain at large. Non-governmental organizations have made similar findings. The Center for Justice & Accountability, established in 1998 with the support of Amnesty International USA, has

4 U.S. Department of State, Initial Report of the United States of America to the U.N. Committee against Torture at para. 6, U.N. Doc. CAT/C/28/Add.5 (1999) [hereinafter "Initial Report of the United States"].

5 While this report emphasizes torture, the analysis and recommendations described herein apply with equal rigor to other serious human rights abuses, including war crimes, crimes against humanity, genocide, extrajudicial killing, and persecution on account of race, religion, nationality, membership in a particular social group, or political opinion.

6 See Noreen Marcus, *INS Arrests 7 Suspected Rights Violators*, SUN-SENTINEL, May 9, 2001, at 7B; Jody A. Benjamin, *INS Arrests 14 in Rights Abuses in Foreign Lands*, SUN-SENTINEL, Nov. 17, 2000, at 1A; Del Quentin Wilber, *Rights Abusers Can Find Haven: U.S. Immigration Law Enables Torturers to Enter, Stay Safe*, BALT. SUN, Aug. 28, 2000, at A1; Robert L. Jackson, *Setting Up a System to Pursue Alleged War Criminals in U.S.*, LOS ANGELES TIMES, Aug. 17, 1999, at A5.

7 *U.S. Deports Honduran Believed to be Former Death Squad Member*, AGENCE FRANCE PRESSE, Jan. 19, 2001.

investigated over 100 cases of alleged human rights abusers in the United States. Of course, these cases are not exhaustive. For each torturer identified, it is likely that many others have eluded detection.[8] Many of these individuals entered the United States by falsifying information on their immigration documents or failing to disclose their background.[9] Others entered legally and overstayed their visas. Some are living here with the tacit approval of the United States Government.[10]

Torture is a gross offense to human dignity, justice, and the rule of law.[11] It is firmly prohibited by international law. It is a crime in all places and at all times. Indeed, torturers are considered *hostis humani generis*—enemies of all humanity. The Convention against Torture and Other Cruel, Inhuman or Degrading Treatment or Punishment requires states to extradite or prosecute individuals found in their territory who allegedly committed acts of torture, regardless of where such acts occurred.[12] The United States accepted this international obligation when it ratified the Convention. Despite this clear moral and legal mandate, perpetrators of human rights abuses continue to enter and reside in the United States with impunity.

---

8 Alfonso Chardy and Elisabeth Donovan, *Scores Accused of Atrocities Committed in Other Countries Are Quietly Living in U.S.*, MIAMI HERALD, July 22, 2001; Andrew Bounds, *U.S. Catches Up with Abusers of Human Rights: The Justice Department Has Begun Rounding Up Immigrants Accused of State-Sponsored Atrocities*, FINANCIAL TIMES (LONDON), May 24, 2001, at 7.

9 However, legitimate refugees also use false documents in seeking to escape persecution. *See* UNHCR, GUIDELINES ON APPLICABLE CRITERIA AND STANDARDS RELATING TO THE DETENTION OF ASYLUM-SEEKERS (1999).

10 *See, e.g.,* Letter from Richard Krieger, International Educational Missions, Inc., to the Honorable John Ashcroft, Attorney General, (April 18, 2001). *See also* David Adams, *Reaching for More Foreign Criminals*, ST. PETERSBURG TIMES, Apr. 9, 2001, at 1A.

11 For recent studies on torture and the international prohibition against torture, see AMNESTY INTERNATIONAL, TORTURE WORLDWIDE: AN AFFRONT TO HUMAN DIGNITY (2000); Winston P. Nagan and Lucie Atkins, *The International Law of Torture: From Universal Proscription to Effective Application and Enforcement*, 14 HARV. HUM. RTS. J. 87 (2001); Winfried Burger, *May Government Ever Use Torture? Two Responses From German Law*, 48 AM. J. COMP. L. 661 (2000).

12 Convention against Torture and Other Cruel, Inhuman or Degrading Treatment or Punishment, Dec. 10, 1984, 1465 U.N.T.S. 85 [hereinafter "Convention against Torture"].

When perpetrators of torture walk the streets with impunity, it is not only their victims who suffer—it is an affront to all humanity. For these reasons, Amnesty International USA has issued this Report examining the presence of torturers from abroad in the United States and the struggle to combat impunity.[13]

What is impunity?

Amnesty International defines impunity as "the failure to bring to justice and punish those responsible for serious violations of human rights and international humanitarian law."[14] Impunity exists at several levels.[15] It exists at the individual level, when perpetrators refuse to acknowledge the wrongfulness of their conduct. It exists at the societal level, when states refuse to accept responsibility for the acts of government agents. And it exists at the international level, when the international community does not respond to human rights abuses.

Impunity occurs for several reasons.[16] On some occasions, countries choose not to prosecute perpetrators. Some of these cases occur when amnesty is provided to perpetrators by the same government that authorized or acquiesced in the human rights abuses. Countries facing turbulent democratic transition may also forego prosecution of past abuses. On other occasions, perpetrators flee their countries, seeking anonymity and absolution in foreign lands.

---

13 This Report focuses exclusively on the presence of torturers from abroad in the United States. It does not address cases of torture that occur in the United States. *See generally* AMNESTY INTERNATIONAL, STOPPING THE TORTURE TRADE (2001); AMNESTY INTERNATIONAL, UNITED STATES OF AMERICA: A BRIEFING FOR THE U.N. COMMITTEE AGAINST TORTURE (2000).

14 AMNESTY INTERNATIONAL, END IMPUNITY: JUSTICE FOR VICTIMS OF TORTURE 14 (2001).

15 *See generally* Question of the Impunity of Perpetrators of Human Rights Violations (Civil and Political), U.N. Doc. E/CN.4/Sub.2/1997/20/Rev.1 (1997); Final Report on the Question of the Impunity of Perpetrators of Human Rights Violations (Economic, Social and Cultural Rights), U.N. Doc. E/CN.4/Sub.2/1997/8 (1997).

16 *See generally* MARTHA MINOW, BETWEEN VENGEANCE AND FORGIVENESS (1998); ARYEH NEIER, WAR CRIMES: BRUTALITY, GENOCIDE, TERROR, AND THE STRUGGLE FOR JUSTICE (1998).

Why combat impunity?

Why should countries take action against individuals who committed human rights abuses abroad? The struggle against impunity serves many purposes.[17]

Individual accountability affirms the normative value of life and upholds respect for human dignity. Torture and other forms of persecution are antithetical to these values, and impunity further undermines them.

Promoting accountability serves as a powerful deterrent against future atrocities. In many countries, gross abuses of human rights often go unpunished. Lack of individual accountability encourages human rights abuses and promotes further disintegration of the rule of law. "Impunity sends the message to torturers that they will get away with it."[18] By pursuing cases against torturers, governments forcefully voice their condemnation of such acts and place future perpetrators on notice. As stated by the International Military Tribunal at Nuremberg, "[c]rimes against international law are committed by men, not by abstract entities, and only by punishing individuals who commit such crimes can the provisions of international law be enforced."[19]

States that pursue cases against torturers also perform the crucial function of distinguishing individual responsibility from group responsibility. Groups identified by certain shared characteristics often receive public blame, both at home and abroad, for the crimes of relatively few offenders. Judge Richard Goldstone, the first prosecutor of the International Criminal Tribunal for the former Yugoslavia, explained this phenomenon in the context of regional human rights abuses: "Too many people

---

17 See generally ACCOUNTABILITY FOR HUMAN RIGHTS ATROCITIES IN INTERNATIONAL LAW (Steven R. Ratner and Jason S. Abrams eds., 1997); Roland Bank, International Efforts to Combat Torture and Inhuman Treatment: Have the New Mechanisms Improved Protection?, 8 EUR. J. INT'L L. 613 (1997); M. Cherif Bassiouni, Accountability for International Crime and Serious Violations of Fundamental Human Rights, 59 LAW & CONTEMP. PROB. 63 (1996); Diane F. Orentlicher, Settling Accounts: The Duty to Prosecute Human Rights Violations of a Prior Regime, 100 YALE L.J. 2537 (1991); Naomi Roht-Arriaza, State Responsibility to Investigate and Prosecute Grave Human Rights Violations in International Law, 78 CAL. L. REV. 449 (1990).

18 AMNESTY INTERNATIONAL, END IMPUNITY, supra, at 6.

19 The Nuremberg Trial, 6 F.R.D. 69, 110 (1946).

in the former Yugoslavia still blame Serbs or Croats or Muslims for their suffering. The tribunal's mandate is to help reverse this destructive legacy."[20] Legal proceedings against torturers focus blame where it belongs, calling individuals to account for their crimes and absolving communal blame.

The struggle against impunity, however, is not limited to punishing perpetrators. It also benefits victims by assuaging their feelings of helplessness and defeat, emotions that often permeate victims of repression. Anti-impunity efforts can also promote reparations for torture victims, including rehabilitation, restitution, and compensation. In the absence of such ameliorative efforts, victims will continue to suffer long after their physical and emotional scars fade from the public conscience. These concerns are particularly relevant for the United States, where it is estimated that over 400,000 torture survivors live.[21]

More broadly, any effort to hold a torturer accountable reinforces human rights values everywhere. Publicity generated by these cases helps to educate the general public about the importance of human rights. These cases also provide support for human rights activists throughout the world. Efforts to hold torturers accountable demonstrate that judicial systems are willing to adjudicate human rights cases and combat impunity.

Finally, promoting accountability encourages the search for truth. By pursuing cases against torturers, a public record is created that describes the human rights abuses committed by the perpetrators and the injustices suffered by the victims. These victims have an opportunity to tell their stories in public, and a fair and full hearing can help restore their sense of justice. Even if victims do not participate, these proceedings can empower them and facilitate their recovery. Indeed, accountability can serve as an important rehabilitative vehicle for perpetrators as well.[22] Such developments can further promote social and political

---

20 Richard J. Goldstone, *Ethnic Reconciliation Needs the Help of a Truth Commission*, INT'L HERALD TRIB., Oct. 24, 1998, at 6.

21 *See* Discretionary Funds for Assistance for Treatment of Torture Survivors, 66 Fed. Reg. 13771 (2001).

22 *See* Mark Andrew Sherman, *Some Thoughts on Restoration, Reintegration, and Justice in the Transnational Context*, 23 FORDHAM INT'L L.J. 1397 (2000).

reconciliation in countries traumatized by periods of repression and persecution.

A multi-track strategy to combat impunity

In the absence of an effective government policy, torturers and other human rights abusers will continue to enter and remain in the United States with impunity. If the United States is a safe haven for these perpetrators, it will undermine its ability to pursue an effective foreign policy premised upon human rights and respect for the rule of law.

Amnesty International USA recommends the following multi-track strategy to combat impunity and ameliorate the consequences of torture and other human rights abuses for victims and their families residing in the United States.[23]

- The United States should investigate any individual located in territory under its jurisdiction alleged to have committed acts of torture.
- The United States should immediately take into custody or take other legal measures to ensure the presence of any individual located in territory under its jurisdiction alleged to have committed acts of torture upon being satisfied after an examination of available information that the circumstances so warrant.
- The United States should extradite any individual located in territory under its jurisdiction alleged to have committed acts of torture if it receives a valid request from a foreign government and it ensures that the individual will not be subject to the death penalty, torture, or other cruel, inhuman or degrading treatment or punishment upon extradition, unless the case is referred to the Justice Department for the purpose of prosecution.
- The United States should surrender any individual located in territory under its jurisdiction alleged to have committed

---

23 These recommendations apply to all acts of torture, including attempts to commit torture as well as acts that constitute complicity or participation in torture.

acts of torture if it receives a valid request from an authorized international court or tribunal.

- The United States should refer the case of any individual located in territory under its jurisdiction alleged to have committed acts of torture to the Justice Department for the purpose of prosecution if extradition or surrender are unavailable or not feasible.
- The United States should limit the scope of immigration relief available to individuals who have committed acts of torture.
- The United States should establish and adequately fund an office within the Justice Department to have primary responsibility for investigating and prosecuting cases of torture and other crimes under international law.
- The United States should increase its support for civil actions filed by victims of torture.
- The United States should increase its support, both at home and abroad, for victims of torture.
- The United States should increase its support for international efforts to combat torture and impunity.

While this Report focuses on the United States, this multi-track strategy should be pursued by all countries. Indeed, a coordinated program to combat impunity through the use of domestic institutions should complement parallel efforts at the international level.[24]

An overview of the report

This Report describes the struggle to combat impunity and pursue accountability in the United States. Part 3 reviews the prevention and punishment of torture under international law. Part 4 describes the concept of universal jurisdiction, which authorizes criminal prosecution for acts of torture. Part 5 examines the problem of torturers from abroad residing in the United States. Several cases are highlighted. Part 6 considers the range of

---

24 *See* William J. Aceves, *Liberalism and International Legal Scholarship: The Pinochet Case and the Move Towards a Universal System of Transnational Law Litigation*, 41 HARV. INT'L L.J. 129 (2000).

options available in the United States for dealing with torturers from abroad: extradition and surrender proceedings, criminal prosecution, civil sanctions, and immigration restrictions. While it is important to develop a cohesive policy that targets perpetrators of human rights abuses, the victims cannot be forgotten. Accordingly, Part 7 considers how to assist victims of torture residing in the United States. Part 8 provides a comparative approach, examining how several countries, including Canada, Belgium, Switzerland, and Spain, have addressed the problem of impunity. Finally, Part 9 proposes several policy recommendations to ensure that the United States does not become a safe haven for perpetrators of human rights atrocities. Respect for human rights, due process, and the rule of law should guide these efforts to combat impunity so that the search for justice is not undermined.

It is unacceptable for states to condemn human rights abuses that take place abroad and yet allow the perpetrators of those abuses to reside in their territory with impunity. The struggle to protect and preserve human rights should always begin at home.

3: The prevention and punishment of torture

"I don't remember those early days and weeks and months very well. The first day, yes. All the rest is blurred. I was unconscious a lot of the time, or I was too weak or too tired. I can only tell you how it all started. There was no real routine to the torture. I didn't know when to expect it or why. When it happened, it was always at night, from nine o'clock to about three in the morning. Perhaps that was when they were bored."

—Saida Botan Elmi
Torture survivor from Somalia[25]

Few international norms are more widely accepted than the prohibition against torture. Torture is generally understood as acts or threatened acts of public officials that intentionally inflict severe physical or mental pain or suffering on an individual in order to fulfill a certain purpose.[26] The prohibition against torture is codified in several multilateral and regional instruments. It is also expressed in numerous other forms of state practice, including the decisions of international and regional tribunals, the statements of international and regional organizations, and in national legislation. Despite such codification efforts, no definition can fully convey the scope and intensity of human suffering caused by torture.

The Convention against Torture

In 1948, the U.N. General Assembly adopted the Universal Declaration of Human Rights ("Universal Declaration"), which is one of the most well-recognized and respected statements of international human rights norms.[27] While the Universal Declaration is not a

25 Amnesty International, Good News (January 6, 1999).

26 *See generally* Sir Nigel S. Rodley, The Treatment of Prisoners under International Law 75-77 (2d ed. 1999).

27 G.A. Res. 217 (A)(III), U.N. Doc. A/810 at 71 (1948).

treaty, it is recognized to embody the rules of international human rights law that all governments are bound to respect. Article 5 of the Universal Declaration clearly states that "no one shall be subjected to torture or to cruel, inhuman or degrading treatment or punishment." Since the adoption of the Universal Declaration, numerous agreements have affirmed this prohibition. For example, the International Covenant on Civil and Political Rights ("ICCPR"), adopted in 1966, codifies many of the rights set forth in the Universal Declaration.[28] Article 7 provides that "[n]o one shall be subjected to torture or to cruel, inhuman or degrading treatment or punishment." The General Assembly reaffirmed the prohibition against torture in its 1975 Declaration on the Protection of all Persons from Being Subjected to Torture and Other Cruel, Inhuman or Degrading Treatment or Punishment.[29]

In 1984, the Convention against Torture was adopted by the U.N. General Assembly.[30] It entered into force on June 26, 1987. The United States ratified the Convention against Torture in October 1994. Currently, 127 states have signed and ratified the Convention.

Defining torture

Article 1 of the Convention against Torture provides in pertinent part:

> "torture" means any act by which severe pain or suffering, whether physical or mental, is intentionally inflicted by or at the instigation of a public official on a person for such purposes as obtaining from him a confession, punishing him for an act he or a third person has committed or

28 International Covenant on Civil and Political Rights, Dec. 16, 1966, 999 U.N.T.S. 171 [hereinafter "ICCPR"]. As of December 28, 2001, there are 147 States Parties to the ICCPR.

29 G.A. Res. 3452 (XXX) (1975).

30 As of December 28, 2001, there are 127 States Parties to the Convention against Torture. An additional eleven states have signed but not ratified the agreement. *See generally* AHCENE BOULESBAA, THE U.N. CONVENTION ON TORTURE AND THE PROSPECTS FOR ENFORCEMENT (1999); J. HERMAN BURGERS AND HANS DANELIUS, THE UNITED NATIONS CONVENTION AGAINST TORTURE: A HANDBOOK ON THE CONVENTION AGAINST TORTURE AND OTHER CRUEL, INHUMAN OR DEGRADING TREATMENT OR PUNISHMENT (1988).

is suspected of having committed, or intimidating or coercing him or a third person, or for any reason based on discrimination of any kind, when such pain or suffering is inflicted by or at the instigation of or with the consent or acquiescence of a public official or other person acting in an official capacity.

Significantly, Article 2(2) provides that "[n]o exceptional circumstances whatsoever, whether a state of war or a threat of war, internal political instability or any other public emergency, may be invoked as a justification of torture." Article 2(3) adds that "[a]n order from a superior officer or a public authority may not be invoked as a justification of torture."

Establishing jurisdiction for acts of torture

Pursuant to Article 2(1) of the Convention against Torture, states must take effective legislative, administrative, and judicial measures to prevent acts of torture in any territory under their jurisdiction.[31] For example, Article 4(1) of the Convention provides that each state party shall ensure that all acts of torture, attempts to commit torture, and acts which constitute complicity or participation in torture, are offenses under their criminal law.[32] These offenses must be punishable by appropriate penalties that take into account their grave nature. In addition, Article 5 requires a state party to establish jurisdiction over these offenses. Specifically, Article 5(1) requires each state party to establish jurisdiction in the following cases: (a) when the offenses are committed in any territory under its jurisdiction or on board a ship or aircraft registered in that state; (b) when the alleged offender is a national of that state; or (c) when the victim is a national of that state if that state considers it appropriate. Article 5(2) requires each state party to establish jurisdiction in

---

31 Convention against Torture, *supra*, at art. 2(1). States are also obligated to prevent in any territory under their jurisdiction other acts of cruel, inhuman or degrading treatment or punishment which do not amount to torture when such acts are committed with the consent or acquiescence of a public official or other person acting in an official capacity. *Id.* at art. 16(1).

32 *Id.* at art. 4(1).

cases where the alleged offender is present in any territory under its jurisdiction and it does not extradite her/him.[33]

The obligation to extradite or prosecute

The Convention against Torture is quite detailed in its description of the state party obligation to investigate persons suspected of torture. Under Article 6(1), a state party in whose territory a person alleged to have committed acts of torture is present shall, upon being satisfied after an examination of information available that the circumstances so warrant, take her/him into custody or take other legal measures to ensure her/his presence. Custody or other legal measures may only be continued for as long as necessary to enable criminal or extradition proceedings to be instituted.[34] The state party must make a preliminary inquiry into the facts of the alleged torture and notify the state where the offenses were committed or where the alleged offender or victim is a national.[35] It must also indicate whether it intends to exercise jurisdiction over the person.

Article 7(1) authorizes a state party to extradite an alleged offender. Under the rule of *non-refoulement*, however, a state party may not extradite a person to another state when there are substantial grounds for believing that he would be in danger of being subjected to torture.[36] For the purpose of determining whether there are such grounds, a state party must take into account all relevant considerations, including the existence of a consistent pattern of gross, flagrant, or mass violations of human rights in the requesting state.[37]

If a state party does not extradite the alleged offender, Article 7(1) requires the state party to submit the case to its competent authorities for prosecution. Decisions on prosecution must be made in the same manner as in the case of any ordinary offense of a serious nature.[38]

---

33 *Id.* at art. 5.

34 *Id.* at 6(1). Throughout custody, a detained individual must be allowed to communicate with a representative of the state where he is a national. *Id.* at art. 6(3).

35 *Id.* at art. 6(4).

36 *Id.* at art. 3(1).

37 *Id.* at art. 3(2).

38 *Id.* at 7(2).

In proceedings initiated under Article 5(2), the standards of evidence required for prosecution and conviction cannot be less stringent than those in other cases. All persons must be guaranteed fair treatment at each stage of the proceedings.[39] The Convention also requires states to provide each other the greatest measure of assistance in connection with criminal proceedings brought in respect to any acts of torture.[40]

The Committee against Torture

To ensure that member states adhere to these provisions, the Convention against Torture established the Committee against Torture.[41] The Committee has several responsibilities. It is authorized to review and comment upon periodic reports submitted by states parties describing their compliance with the Convention against Torture.[42] The Committee is also authorized to receive state and individual communications alleging noncompliance by states parties.[43] In these cases, however, the target state must have previously accepted the competence of the Committee to review these communications. Although the United States is obligated to submit periodic reports to the Committee and has accepted its competence to receive and consider state communications, it has not accepted the competence of the Committee to review individual communications.

The U.N. Special Rapporteur on Torture

Apart from the Convention against Torture and its constituent Committee against Torture, several other agreements and entities

---

39 *Id.* at 7(3).

40 *Id.* at art. 9.

41 *Id.* at art. 17. *See generally* Peter Burns, *The United Nations Committee against Torture and its Role in Refugee Protection*, 15 GEO. IMMIGR. L.J. 403 (2001).

42 Convention against Torture, *supra*, at art. 19. In October 1999, the United States issued its Initial Report to the Committee against Torture.

43 *Id.* at art. 21, art. 22.

are relevant to the international campaign against torture.[44] Perhaps the most prominent of these is the U.N. Special Rapporteur on the question of torture, which was established by the Commission on Human Rights in 1985.[45] The Special Rapporteur's mandate is to investigate reports of torture and make urgent appeals to governments in cases where a person is at risk of being subjected to torture.[46] In 1999, the U.N. Special Rapporteur indicated that "the phenomenon of torture continues to plague all regions of the world."[47] Significantly, the Special Rapporteur found that "impunity continues to be the principal cause of the perpetuation and encouragement of human rights violations and, in particular, torture."[48]

*****

In sum, the international community recognizes that acts of torture cannot be tolerated under any circumstances. This universal condemnation has led the international community to place torture in that narrow realm of *jus cogens* norms—nonderogable obligations that bind all states.[49] The crime of torture is recognized both under the Convention against Torture and under customary international law to be subject to universal jurisdiction—states are authorized to prosecute an alleged torturer located in their territory regardless of where the act of torture

---

44 In addition to multilateral agreements, the prohibition against torture is recognized in several regional agreements. *See* European Convention for the Protection of Human Rights and Fundamental Freedoms, Nov. 4, 1950, art. 3, 213 U.N.T.S. 222 ("No one shall be subjected to torture or to inhuman or degrading treatment or punishment."); American Convention on Human Rights, Nov. 22, 1969, art. 5(2), O.A.S.T.S. No. 36 ("No one shall be subjected to torture or to cruel, inhuman or degrading punishment or treatment."); African Charter on Human and Peoples' Rights, June 26, 1981, art. 5, OAU Doc. CAB/LEG/67/3/Rev. ("All forms of exploitation and degradation of man particularly slavery, slave trade, torture, cruel, inhuman or degrading punishment and treatment shall be prohibited.").

45 Commission on Human Rights Resolution 1985/33 (1985).

46 *See, e.g.*, Report of the Special Rapporteur, Sir Nigel Rodley, Submitted Pursuant to Commission on Human Rights Resolution 1999/32, U.N. Doc. E/CN.4/2000/9 (2000).

47 Report on Torture and other Cruel, Inhuman or Degrading Treatment or Punishment, Submitted by Sir Nigel Rodley, Special Rapporteur of the Commission on Human Rights, in Accordance with General Assembly Resolution 53/139, U.N. Doc. A/54/426 (1999).

48 *Id.*

49 *See generally* LAURI HANNIKAINEN, PEREMPTORY NORMS IN INTERNATIONAL LAW: HISTORICAL DEVELOPMENT, CRITERIA, PRESENT STATUS (1988); CHRISTOS L. ROZAKIS, THE CONCEPT OF JUS COGENS IN INTERNATIONAL LAW (1976).

took place.[50] Indeed, the Convention against Torture expressly requires states to take such action against any suspect in territory under their jurisdiction if they do not extradite the suspect and the circumstances warrant. These principles have been recognized by various bodies, from the International Criminal Tribunal for the former Yugoslavia to the British House of Lords.[51]

---

50 The Committee against Torture has indicated that "even before the entry into force of the Convention against Torture, there existed a general rule of international law which should oblige all States to take effective measures to prevent torture and to punish acts of torture." Report of the Committee against Torture, U.N. GAOR, 45th Sess., Supp. No. 44, Annex V, para. 7.2, U.N. Doc. A/45/44 (1990). *See generally* AMNESTY INTERNATIONAL, UNIVERSAL JURISDICTION: 14 PRINCIPLES ON THE EFFECTIVE EXERCISE OF UNIVERSAL JURISDICTION (1999); INTERNATIONAL COUNCIL ON HUMAN RIGHTS POLICY, HARD CASES: BRINGING HUMAN RIGHTS VIOLATORS TO JUSTICE ABROAD (1999); AMNESTY INTERNATIONAL, THE PINOCHET CASE—UNIVERSAL JURISDICTION AND THE ABSENCE OF IMMUNITY FOR CRIMES AGAINST HUMANITY (1999). *See also* William J. Aceves, *Liberalism and International Legal Scholarship: The Pinochet Case and the Move Toward a Universal System of Transnational Law Litigation,* 41 HARV. INT'L L.J. 129 (2000); Damien Vandermeersch, *La répression en droit belge des crimes de droit international,* 68 INT'L REV. PENAL L. (1997); Luc Reydams, *Universal Jurisdiction over Atrocities in Rwanda: Theory and Practice,* 4 EUR. J. CRIME, CRIM. L. & CRIM. JUST. 18 (1996); Jeffrey Rabkin, *Universal Justice: The Role of Federal Courts in International Civil Litigation,* 95 COLUM. L. REV. 2120 (1995); Kenneth Randall, *Universal Jurisdiction Under International Law,* 66 TEXAS L. REV. 785 (1988); Rena Hozore Reis, *The Extradition of John Demjanjuk: War Crimes, Universal Jurisdiction, and the Political Offense Doctrine,* 20 CORNELL INT'L L.J. 281 (1987).

51 *See* Prosecutor v. Anton Furundzjia, International Criminal Tribunal for the former Yugoslavia, (Dec. 10, 1998), para. 156, *reprinted in* 38 I.L.M. 346 (1999). *See* R v. Bow Street Metropolitan Stipendiary Magistrate, *ex parte* Pinochet Ugarte (Amnesty International and others intervening) (No. 3), 2 All E.R. 97 (H.L. 1999) [hereinafter "Ex parte Pinochet"].

4: The concept of universal jurisdiction

"What we are really searching for is some truth."
—Zita Cabello-Barrueto[52]
One of the surviving family members who filed
a lawsuit in a U.S. court against a former Chilean
army major who allegedly tortured and executed
Winston Cabello

Under international law, states may acquire jurisdiction over individuals in several ways.[53] Perhaps the most common form is territorial jurisdiction, which recognizes state jurisdiction for any acts committed within its own territory.[54] Another common form of jurisdiction is the active personality, or nationality, principle, which recognizes a state's jurisdiction for any acts committed by the nationals of that state. In addition, the passive personality principle recognizes state jurisdiction for any acts committed against a state's own nationals. Each of these principles of jurisdiction is premised upon an explicit relationship between the state and a particular individual.[55] This relationship justifies the imposition of state jurisdiction.

In contrast, the principle of universal jurisdiction recognizes state jurisdiction even in the absence of one of these explicit relationships.[56] One rationale for such jurisdiction is that

---

52 See *infra* Section 5. David Kidwell, *Chilean's Survivors Sue Miami Businessman,* MIAMI HERALD, March, 23, 1999.

53 See generally IAN BROWNLIE, PRINCIPLES OF PUBLIC INTERNATIONAL LAW 300-05 (4th ed. 1990).

54 According to Ian Brownlie, "[t]he principle that the courts of the place where the crime is committed may exercise jurisdiction has received universal recognition, and is but a single application of the essential territoriality of the sovereign, the sum of legal competences, which a state has." *Id.* at 300.

55 *See* PETER MALANCZUK, AKEHURST'S MODERN INTRODUCTION TO INTERNATIONAL LAW 109-15 (7th ed. 1997); BRANIMIR M. JANKOVIC, PUBLIC INTERNATIONAL LAW 2-4 (1984).

56 *See generally* PRINCETON UNIVERSITY, PROGRAM IN LAW AND PUBLIC AFFAIRS, THE PRINCETON PRINCIPLES ON UNIVERSAL JURISDICTION (2001); Symposium, *Universal Jurisdiction: Myths, Realities, and Prospects,* 35 NEW ENG. L. REV. 227 (2001). For criticisms of universal jurisdiction, see HENRY KISSINGER, DOES AMERICA NEED A FOREIGN POLICY? 273 (2001); Clive Nicholls, *Reflections on Pinochet,* 41 VA. J. INT'L L. 140 (2000).

violations of international law injure all states.[57] Accordingly, all states have the authority to prosecute these violations regardless of where they took place.[58] One U.S. court has justified the application of universal jurisdiction in the following manner: "[N]either the nationality of the accused or the victim(s), nor the location of the crime is significant. The underlying assumption is that the crimes are offenses against the law of nations or against humanity and that the prosecuting nation is acting for all nations."[59] In these cases, perpetrators of human rights violations are considered *hostis humani generis*—enemies of all humanity.[60] In a similar fashion, the International Court of Justice has recognized that some obligations are the concern of all states, including the prohibition against genocide, slavery, and racial discrimination.[61] "In view of the importance of the rights involved, all states can be held

---

57 The importance of establishing universal jurisdiction for certain violations of international law was indicated in the final report *Question of the Impunity of Perpetrators of Human Rights Violations* submitted to the Sub-Commission on Prevention of Discrimination and Protection of Minorities of the U.N. Commission on Human Rights by Special Rapporteur Louis Joinet. *Question of the Impunity of Perpetrators of Human Rights Violations*, U.N. ESCOR, 49th Sess., U.N. Doc. E/CN.4/Sub.2/1997/20 (1997). The report identified two ways of establishing universal jurisdiction. First, "[a] provision on universal jurisdiction applicable to serious crimes under international law should be included in all international human rights instruments dealing with such crimes." *Id.* at Principle 24(a). By ratifying such instruments, states would be obligated to seek and prosecute individuals who have violated these human rights agreements. Second, in the absence of an international agreement, "states may for efficiency's sake take measures in their internal legislation to establish extraterritorial jurisdiction over serious crimes under international law . . . ." *Id.* at Principle 25.

58 Brownlie notes that "[a] considerable number of states have adopted, usually with limitations, a principle allowing jurisdiction over acts of non-nationals where the circumstances, including the nature of the crime, justify the repression of some types of crime as a matter of international public policy." BROWNLIE, *supra*, at 304. *See generally* Kenneth C. Randall, *Universal Jurisdiction Under International Law*, 66 TEX. L. REV. 785 (1988); Michael Akehurst, *Jurisdiction in International Law*, 46 BR. YB. INT'L L. 145 (1972–3); Harvard Research on International Law, *Jurisdiction with Respect to Crime*, 29 AM. J. INT'L L. 435 (Supp. 1935).

59 Demjanjuk v. Petrovsky, 776 F.2d 571, 582-83 (6th Cir. 1985).

60 *See* J.L. BRIERLY, THE LAW OF NATIONS: AN INTRODUCTION TO THE INTERNATIONAL LAW OF PEACE 311 (6th ed. 1963). *See also* A. Hays Butler, *The Doctrine of Universal Jurisdiction*, 11 CRIM. L.F. 353 (2000).

61 Case Concerning the Barcelona Traction, Light and Power Company Limited, (Belg. v. Spain), 1970 ICJ REP. 3, 32 (Feb. 5). *See generally* NINA H.B. JØRGENSEN, THE RESPONSIBILITY OF STATES FOR INTERNATIONAL CRIMES 93 (2000); MAURIZIO RAGAZZI, THE CONCEPT OF INTERNATIONAL OBLIGATIONS ERGA OMNES (1997).

to have a legal interest in their protection; they are obligations *erga omnes*."[62]

Several crimes under international law are subject to universal jurisdiction.[63] For example, the 1949 Geneva Conventions indicate that states parties have an obligation to search for persons alleged to have committed grave breaches and to bring such persons, regardless of nationality, before their courts.[64] Grave breaches include such acts as murder, torture, or other cruel, humiliating or degrading treatment committed during international armed conflict. Indeed, states are obligated to search for persons alleged to have committed, or ordered to have committed, such grave breaches. The International Convention against the Taking of Hostages, the Convention on the Prevention and Punishment of Crimes Against Internationally Protected Persons, the Convention for the Suppression of Unlawful Acts against the Safety of Civil Aviation, and the Convention for the Suppression of Unlawful Seizure of Aircraft provide that member states must establish jurisdiction when an alleged offender is present in their territory, regardless of nationality.[65]

The Convention against Torture also recognizes universal jurisdiction under its extradite or prosecute (*aut dedere aut judicaire*) regime. Article 5(2) requires each state party to establish

---

62 Case Concerning the Barcelona Traction, Light and Power Company Limited, *supra*, at 32. According to the International Law Commission, "the responsibility engaged by the breach of these obligations is engaged not only in regard to the state which was the direct victim of the breach: it is also engaged in regard to all the other members of the international community, so that, in the event of a breach of these obligations every state must be considered justified in invoking—probably through judicial channels—the responsibility of the state committing the internationally wrongful act." [1976] Y.B. INT'L L. COMM'N, pt. 2, 99.

63 Universal jurisdiction is also recognized for such crimes as genocide, hijacking, piracy, slavery, and crimes against humanity. *See generally* RESTATEMENT (THIRD) OF THE FOREIGN RELATIONS LAW OF THE UNITED STATES § 404 (1987) [hereinafter "RESTATEMENT (THIRD)"].

64 *See, e.g.*, Geneva Convention Relative to the Treatment of Prisoners of War, Aug. 12, 1949, art. 129, 75 U.N.T.S. 135, 6 U.S.T. 3316.

65 *See generally* International Convention against the Taking of Hostages, Dec. 17, 1979, art. 5, T.I.A.S. No. 11,081, 1316 U.N.T.S. 205; Convention on the Prevention and Punishment of Crimes Against Internationally Protected Persons, Including Diplomatic Agents, Dec. 14, 1973, art. 3, T.I.A.S. No. 8532, 1035 U.N.T.S. 167; Convention for the Suppression of Unlawful Acts against the Safety of Civil Aviation, Sept. 23, 1971, art. 5, 564 T.I.A.S. No. 564, 974 U.N.T.S. 177; Convention for the Suppression of Unlawful Seizure of Aircraft, Dec. 16, 1970, art. 4, T.I.A.S. No. 7192, 860 U.N.T.S. 105.

jurisdiction in cases where the alleged offender is present in any territory under its jurisdiction and it does not extradite her/him. If a person alleged to have committed acts of torture is found in the territory of a state party, it is obligated under Article 6(1) to investigate and, where appropriate, to take her/him into custody or take other legal measures to ensure her/his presence. Article 7(1) authorizes a state party to extradite an alleged offender. If a state party does not extradite the alleged offender, Article 7(1) requires the state party to submit the case to its competent authorities for prosecution. Each facet of the Convention against Torture acknowledges the relevance of universal jurisdiction and the concomitant obligation of states parties to combat impunity. The obligation to extradite or prosecute helps to ensure that individuals who violate the prohibition against torture are brought to justice. As noted by Lord Hope in the Pinochet case, the international prohibition against torture "compels all states to refrain from such conduct under any circumstances and imposes an obligation *erga omnes* to punish such conduct."[66]

The principle of universal jurisdiction is not limited to criminal prosecution.[67] Some states have extended the application of universal jurisdiction to civil proceedings. For example, universal jurisdiction has been used to authorize tort remedies for victims of human rights violations.[68] As indicated by the U.S. Senate, "[s]tates have the option, under international law, to decide whether they will allow a private right of action in their courts for violations of human rights that take place abroad."[69] This interpretation is consistent with the Convention against Torture, which requires states to ensure that their legal systems provide redress and an enforceable right to fair and adequate compensation for torture victims.[70]

66 Ex parte Pinochet, *supra*, at 881 (Hope, L.).

67 *See generally* David Bederman et. al., *The Enforcement of Human Rights and Humanitarian Law By Civil Suits in Municipal Courts: The Civil Dimension of Universal Jurisdiction, reprinted in* CONTEMPORARY INTERNATIONAL LAW ISSUES: NEW FORMS, NEW APPLICATIONS 156 (Wybo P. Here ed., 1998).

68 RESTATEMENT (THIRD), *supra*, § 404, cmt. b.

69 S. Rep. No. 102-249, at 3 (1991).

70 Convention against Torture, *supra*, at art. 14.

5: Torturers in our midst: an overview of the problem

*"It is really appalling to think that the United States
has become the retirement home of choice for murderers
and despots."*

—William P. Ford[71]
    **Brother of one of four American women killed
    by members of the Salvadoran National Guard
    in 1980**

The universal condemnation of torture, rooted in respect for
human dignity and integrity, stands in stark contrast to the
realities of today's world. Since 1997, Amnesty International has
received reports of torture and ill-treatment inflicted by state
agents in over 150 countries.[72]

Equally widespread, and equally alarming, is the almost
complete failure of governments throughout the world to
bring torturers to justice. Amnesty International's research
has repeatedly demonstrated that the number of criminal
investigations, prosecutions, and convictions involving cases
of torture bears no relation to the frequency with which
torture is committed. In 1999, the U.N. Special Rapporteur
on torture noted that "statistical information provided by
both government officials and non-governmental organizations demonstrates that very few allegations lead to prosecutions."[73] The United States is no exception. Not a single
prosecution has been initiated since Congress adopted legislation in 1994 criminalizing acts of torture committed outside the
United States.

---

71 *See* Steve Fainaru, *U.S. is a Haven for Suspected War Criminals*, BOSTON GLOBE, May 2, 1999, at A1.

72 *See generally* AMNESTY INTERNATIONAL, TAKE A STEP TO STAMP OUT TORTURE (2001); AMNESTY INTERNATIONAL, TORTURE WORLDWIDE: AN AFFRONT TO HUMAN DIGNITY (2000).

73 UN Doc. E/CN.4/1999/61/Add.1, 27 January 1999, paragraph 72.

An initial accounting

There is no precise figure on the number of alleged torturers and other perpetrators of human rights abuses residing in the United States. This is not surprising in light of the impediments to identifying and tracking suspected perpetrators. First, these individuals generally do not publicize their presence or past actions that might be considered criminal. Second, immigrant communities rarely report suspected human rights abusers because they fear reprisals and are skeptical that coming forward will result in the perpetrators being brought to justice.[74] Third, the U.S. Government only recently began investigating modern-day human rights abusers in the United States.[75]

There are, however, a number of sources that, taken together, begin to reveal the scope of the problem.

In 1998, the Center for Justice & Accountability ("CJA") was established with support from Amnesty International USA and the United Nations Voluntary Fund for Victims of Torture. CJA investigates cases of suspected perpetrators of torture and other serious human rights violations who live in or visit the United States. It files civil lawsuits on behalf of torture survivors and their families in U.S. courts. It also encourages criminal prosecution, extradition, or other appropriate action against suspected torturers. Since its founding, CJA has investigated over 100 cases of alleged human rights abusers residing in the United States. These cases have involved individuals from various countries, including Afghanistan, Bosnia, Cambodia, Chile, El Salvador, Guatemala, Haiti, Indonesia, Iraq, Nicaragua, Sierra Leone, and Vietnam. CJA has referred approximately 10 of these cases to the Justice Department for further investigation.

The International Educational Missions ("IEM"), which was established in 1987, has investigated more than 150 cases of suspected torturers residing in the United States, particularly

74 Gerald Gray, The Number of Human Rights Criminals in the United States and the Implications for the Torture Treatment Movement (2001) (unpublished manuscript).

75 In contrast, the Office of Special Investigations in the Department of Justice has been tracking cases of Nazi war criminals since 1979.

in southern Florida.[76] It has referred some 50 cases to the Department of Justice. As of January 2002, IEM estimates that approximately 1,100 human rights abusers are now in the United States.[77]

In 1997, the INS established the National Security Unit ("NSU") within the Investigations Division of the Office of Field Operations.[78] In 1998, the NSU took on the task of coordinating investigations into suspected human rights abusers.[79] Since that time, the NSU has investigated approximately 400 such cases.[80] The NSU's Director acknowledges, however, that the actual number of suspected human rights abusers residing in the United States may be as high as 800–1,000.[81]

The INS has conducted two well-publicized sweeps targeting suspected human rights persecutors. On November 15, 2000, the INS executed Operation Home Run, a tactical action designed to locate, detain, and deport aliens living in the United States who allegedly committed human rights abuses in foreign countries.[82] Throughout southern Florida, INS agents located and detained 14 aliens suspected of committing abuses in their home countries,

---

76 See, e.g., Andrew Bounds, U.S. Catches Up With Abusers of Human Rights, FINANCIAL TIMES (LONDON), May 24, 2001, at 7; Niles Lathem, Nazi Hunter is on Their Trail, NEW YORK POST, May 31, 2001, at 7.

77 Alfonso Chardy, Nazi Hunter on Quest to Expel Other 'Torturers,' MIAMI HERALD, March 15, 2001; Bill Douthat, Boyton-Area Man Tracks, Ousts Torturers, PALM BEACH POST, March 21, 2001, at A1.

78 In addition, the Justice Department has designated the Terrorism and Violent Crimes Section in its Criminal Division to investigate cases of human rights abuses. To promote cooperation between these various agencies, the INS and the Federal Bureau of Investigation signed a Memorandum of Understanding ("MOU") regarding the investigation and prosecution of human rights abuse crimes. According to a Justice Department official, "[t]he MOU promotes the effective and efficient investigation and prosecution of human rights abuses by setting out the procedures to be followed and the respective responsibilities of each agency." Adopted Orphans Citizenship Act and Anti-Atrocity Alien Deportation Act: Hearing Before the Subcommittee on Immigration and Claims of the Committee on the Judiciary, House of Representatives, 106th Cong., 1st Sess. 21, 23 (2000) (statement of James Castello, Associate Deputy Attorney General, U.S. Department of State) [hereinafter "Castello Testimony"].

79 Letter from Walter D. Cadman, Director, National Security Unit, Immigration and Naturalization Service to William F. Schulz, Executive Director, Amnesty International USA (September 6, 2001).

80 Interview by Vienna Colucci of Amnesty International USA with Walter D. Cadman, Director, National Security Unit, Immigration and Naturalization Service (August 14, 2001).

81 Id.

82 Press Release, INS Special Agents Arrest Human Rights Persecutors (Nov. 28, 2000).

including Angola, Haiti, and Peru. On May 16, 2001, the INS detained an additional seven aliens as part of Operation Home Run II.[83] By some accounts, there are approximately 140 similar cases in Florida alone.[84]

In addition to the cases investigated by the INS and the above-mentioned NGOs, a number of suspected human rights abusers have also been identified through the growing body of investigative reporting on this topic.[85] Amnesty International USA's review of these cases and of the cases brought to the organization's attention by other sources reveals that nearly 150 suspected human rights abusers are reported to be living in the United States, though the actual number may be substantially higher.

Selected case studies

The following case studies involve individuals who are alleged to be responsible for human rights abuses in their countries of origin and who managed to enter, and in some cases even establish residence in, the United States. Each case reveals flaws in U.S. policy and calls into question the U.S Government's commitment to fulfilling its obligation under international law to bring suspected human rights abusers to justice.

Kelbessa Negewo

From 1974 to 1991, Ethiopia was ruled by a military government known as the "Dergue."[86] During a campaign of repression, political opponents were threatened, tortured, and summarily executed

---

83 Noreen Marcus, *INS Arrests 7 Suspected Rights Violators*, Sun-Sentinel, May 9, 2001, at 7B.

84 Jody Benjamin, *INS Nabs Suspected Torturer*, Sun-Sentinel, June 22, 2001, at 2B.

85 *See generally* Thuy-Doan Le and Daniel Yi, *INS Investigating Allegation Against Vietnam Refugee*, Los Angeles Times, June 12, 2001, at B7; Steve Fainaru, *INS Moves to Track Down Rights Abusers*, Boston Globe, Sept. 20, 1999, at A1; Robert L. Jackson, *Setting Up a System to Pursue Alleged War Criminals in U.S.*, Los Angeles Times, Aug. 17, 1999, at A5; Steve Fainaru, *Suspect in "Cleansing" By Serbs Living in Vt.*, Boston Globe, May 3, 1999, at A1; Steve Fainaru, *U.S. is a Haven for Suspected War Criminals*, Boston Globe, May 2, 1999, at A1.

86 *See generally* Amnesty International, Ethiopia—Accountability Past and Present: Human Rights in Transition (1995); Alexander De Waal, Evil Days: Thirty Years of War and Famine in Ethiopia (1991).

by military and paramilitary groups throughout the country. At the time, Edgegayehu Taye was 21 years old and worked at the Ministry of Agriculture in Addis Ababa. Her father had been a prominent government official under the prior regime of Haile Selassie.

In a complaint filed in U.S. District Court for the Northern District of Georgia, Taye alleges that on February 13, 1978, she was arrested and taken to the local detention facility controlled by Kelbessa Negewo, a government official.[87] At the detention facility, she was ordered to remove her clothes. Her arms and legs were bound, and she was suspended from a pole. She was repeatedly threatened with death if she did not cooperate and disclose her membership in an opposition group. Taye alleges that she was severely beaten by Negewo and several guards, who poured water on the wounds to increase her pain. Taye further alleges that she was interrogated and tortured in Negewo's presence for several hours and that when Negewo grew tired of the interrogation, he ordered the guards to cut Taye loose from the pole and take her to a prison cell. She received no medical care for her wounds. Taye was subsequently transferred to other prison facilities in Addis Ababa. After three years of detention, she was finally released without ever being charged with an offense or brought before a court.

After escaping to Canada and receiving Canadian citizenship, Taye moved to Atlanta, Georgia. While working in an Atlanta hotel, she discovered that Negewo had not only entered the United States as a refugee, but was also working at the same hotel. In September 1990, Taye, along with two other Ethiopian women, Hirut Abebe-Jiri and Elizabeth Demissie, filed a lawsuit against Negewo pursuant to the Alien Tort Claims Act.[88] The plaintiffs alleged that Negewo had ordered and participated in numerous acts of torture and other cruel, inhuman, and degrading treatment against them while they lived in Ethiopia.[89]

---

87 *See generally* Abebe-Jiri v. Negewo, No. 1:90-CV-2010-GET, 1993 WL 814304 (N.D.Ga. Aug. 20, 1993) *aff'd* 72 F.3d 844 (1996).

88 The Alien Tort Claims Act, 28 U.S.C. §1350, provides federal district courts with subject matter jurisdiction over tort actions filed by aliens alleging violations of international law.

89 Complaint, Abebe-Jiri v. Negewo, Case No. 1:90-cv-2010-GET (N.D. GA. Sept. 13, 1990).

In *Abebe-Jiri v. Negewo*, the District Court found Negewo liable for human rights violations.[90] In its findings of fact, the District Court concluded that Negewo had participated in numerous acts of torture. "Defendant Negewo was directly involved in the interrogation and torture of each of the plaintiffs in this case. He was personally present during part of the time they were tortured and supervised at least part of the torture."[91] Based upon these findings, the District Court concluded that Negewo had committed acts of torture and other cruel, inhuman, or degrading treatment. Accordingly, the Court awarded the plaintiffs compensatory and punitive damages in the amount of $1.5 million. The Court of Appeals for the Eleventh Circuit affirmed the District Court's ruling.[92]

While these civil proceedings were pending, Negewo's application for naturalization was under review by the Immigration and Naturalization Service. Although the INS was apparently informed of the District Court's judgment, it approved Negewo's application and granted him U.S. citizenship.[93]

Nikola Vukovic

In 1991, before the breakup of the former Yugoslavia, the municipality of Bosanski Samac, located in northeastern Bosnia-Herzegovina, was populated by over 30,000 people. Almost 17,000 residents were Bosnian Muslims or Croats. Like other municipalities in northeastern Bosnia-Herzegovina, Bosanski Samac held strategic importance for the Bosnian Serb military. Through intimidation, forced displacement, torture, and summary execution, the Bosnian Serbian army gained control over the town and established a Bosnian Serb-controlled corridor in northeastern Bosnia-Herzegovina. By mid-1995, fewer than 300 Bosnian Muslims and Croats remained in Bosanski Samac.

Kemal Mehinovic, a Bosnian Muslim, lived with his wife and two children in Bosanski Samac. According to a complaint filed in U.S.

90 Abebe-Jiri v. Negewo, No. 1:90-CV-2010-GET, 1993 WL 814304 (N.D.Ga. Aug. 20, 1993) aff'd 72 F.3d 844 (1996).

91 *Id.* at 6-7.

92 *See* Abebe-Jiri v. Negewo, 72 F.3d 844 (11th Cir. 1996).

93 *See How a Torture Figure Becomes a Victim*, FULTON COUNTY DAILY REPORT, March 2, 1998.

District Court for the Northern District of Georgia, Mehinovic alleges that on May 27, 1992, Bosnian Serb police officials arrested him at his home and beat him as his family watched helplessly.[94] Mehinovic was then taken to the local police headquarters, where he alleges he was interrogated and regularly beaten for two months. According to the complaint, Nikola Vukovic and other Bosnian Serb soldiers repeatedly beat Mehinovic and other Muslim prisoners, sometimes into unconsciousness, using metal pipes, wooden batons, and their fists.[95] Mehinovic alleges that during one torture session, Vukovic forced him to lick his own blood off the police station wall. During other sessions, Vukovic reportedly made derogatory remarks against Muslims, declaring at one point that "[n]o more Muslims should be born."[96] Mehinovic repeatedly suffered injuries to his head, ribs, and hands. He received

Nikola Vukovic, former Bosnian Serb soldier named in a lawsuit filed in 1998 under the Alien Tort Claims Act and Torture Victim Protection Act.

no medical attention. Psychological torture accompanied the physical acts of torture. Mehinovic alleges that on several occasions Vukovic and other guards or soldiers gathered prisoners in a large room and opened fired around them.[97] The bullets never hit them, but the prisoners remained terrified of imminent death. On one occasion, Vukovic allegedly aimed directly at Mehinovic and shot a bullet just above his head. In July 1992, Mehinovic was transferred to a Territorial Defense military building in Bosanski Samac, where he was held with approximately 300 men. Along with inadequate drinking water and food, the men were given rations containing pork, a meat prohibited by Muslim religious practice. Mehinovic alleges that Vukovic also appeared at the warehouse, where he

94 The allegations against Vukovic are based upon a civil complaint filed in U.S. District Court for the Northern District of Georgia and on testimony presented at the trial. *See* First Amended Complaint, Mehinovic v. Vukovic, Case No. 1 98-CV.2470 (N.D. GA. Dec. 14, 1998). Mehinovic was represented by the Center for Justice & Accountability.

95 *Id.* at 11.

96 *Id.* at 10.

97 *Id.*

beat Mehinovic and other prisoners.[98] After surviving for almost four months in the warehouse, Mehinovic was transferred to a concentration camp east of Bosanski Samac and then to other detention and labor centers in Bosnia-Herzegovina.

On October 6, 1994, after two and a half years of detention, Mehinovic was released in a prisoner exchange near Sarajevo.[99] After searching for several days, he was reunited with his family in Croatia. In July 1995, Mehinovic left Croatia and traveled to the United States with the assistance of the U.S. Government and refugee relief organizations. He was subsequently granted permanent residence in the United States. Ironically, Vukovic also entered the United States as a refugee in October 1997 and settled with his family in a suburb of Atlanta.[100]

In 1998, Mehinovic discovered that Vukovic was living in the United States. In August 1998, Mehinovic filed a lawsuit against Vukovic pursuant to the Alien Tort Claims Act and the Torture Victim Protection Act, which authorize civil actions for acts of torture.[101] Three other Bosnian men allegedly victimized by Vukovic subsequently joined Mehinovic as plaintiffs.[102] The complaint charges Vukovic with numerous violations of international law arising from his actions in Bosnia-Herzegovina. Specifically, the plaintiffs allege that Vukovic is liable for genocide, war crimes, crimes against humanity, torture, cruel and inhumane treatment, and arbitrary detention.[103] In September 1999, the District Court denied Vukovic's motion to dismiss the lawsuit.[104] A bench trial was held in October

---

98 *Id.*

99 *Id.* at 13.

100 *See generally* Brent Israelsen, *Judge Won't Drop Suit Accusing Serb of Torture*, SALT LAKE TRIBUNE, Sept. 17, 1999, at B2.

101 For an overview of the Alien Tort Claims Act and Torture Victim Protection Act, see *infra*, Section 6.

102 The complaint was subsequently amended in December 1998.

103 In 1998, Stevan Todorovic, a former police chief for Bosanki Samac, was indicted by the International Criminal Tribunal for the former Yugoslavia. *See* Chris Stephen, *Bosnian Serb War Crimes Suspect Seized*, THE SCOTSMAN, Sept. 28, 1998, at 7. In December 2000, Todorovic pled guilty to one count of crimes against humanity. *See 12-Year Sentence for Bosnian Serb War Crimes Suspect*, AGENCE FRANCE PRESSE, May 4, 2001. In August 2001, he was sentenced to 10 years in prison (with credit for two years, 10 months' time served). Brent Israelsen, *War Crimes Verdict Brings Relief*, SALT LAKE TRIBUNE, Aug. 2, 2001, at A1.

104 Order, Mehinovic v. Vukovic, Case No. 1 98-CV.2470 (N.D. GA. Sept. 9, 1999).

2001, where the District Court heard testimony from each of the four plaintiffs. Neither Vukovic nor his counsel appeared at trial. A final ruling is now pending.

Tomás Ricardo Anderson Kohatsu

In 1997, two Peruvian army intelligence officers, Leonor La Rosa and Mariela Lucy Barreto, were detained for allegedly leaking government information to opposition groups.[105] La Rosa and Barreto were placed in army detention cells and repeatedly beaten and tortured with electrical shocks. La Rosa required months of hospitalization and rehabilitation, and she remains a paraplegic.[106] Barreto was killed; her dismembered body was ultimately recovered by Peruvian authorities. Several officers from Peru's Army Intelligence Services, including Tomás Ricardo Anderson Kohatsu, were accused of committing these acts. While Anderson Kohatsu was prosecuted and convicted by a military court for misuse of authority, the conviction was subsequently overturned by Peru's Supreme Council of Military Justice.[107] The case received international attention and was raised before the Inter-American Commission on Human

Retired Peruvian army major Tomás Ricardo Anderson Kohatsu, who is accused of torture, at Ronald Reagan National Airport in Washington, DC, on March 9, 2000. Anderson Kohatsu was questioned by the Justice Department later that day in Houston, Texas, but was allowed to return to Peru after the State Department intervened and asserted that Anderson Kohatsu was entitled to diplomatic immunity.

---

105 *See generally* Sean Murphy, *Immunity Provided Peruvian Charged with Torture,* 94 AM. J. INT'L L. 535 (2000); *State Dept. Helped Peruvian Accused of Torture Avoid Arrest,* NEW YORK TIMES, March 11, 2000, at A7; Karen DeYoung and Lorraine Adams, *U.S. Frees Accused Torturer; Human Rights Groups Decry Ruling on Peruvian,* WASH. POST, March 11, 2000, at A1.

106 La Rosa was awarded approximately $1,500 as an indemnity by the Supreme Council of Military Justice. *See* U.S. DEPARTMENT OF STATE, COUNTRY REPORTS ON HUMAN RIGHTS PRACTICES FOR 1999 (2000). In February 2002, the Peruvian government issued a formal apology and $120,000 in compensation to La Rosa. See *Peru Compensates Tortured Ex-Agent,* ASSOCIATED PRESS, February 18, 2002.

107 *Four Army Officers in Torture Case Sentenced to Eight Years in Prison,* BBC, May 12, 1997, LEXIS, Nexis Library, News, Archnws File; U.S. DEPARTMENT OF STATE, COUNTRY REPORTS ON HUMAN RIGHTS PRACTICES FOR 1997, at 625 (1998).

Rights and described in the U.S. State Department's annual
Country Reports on Human Rights Practices.[108]

In early March 2000, Anderson Kohatsu was granted a visa for
the purpose of allowing him to testify before the Inter-American
Commission on Human Rights in Washington, D.C.[109] When several
human rights groups discovered that Anderson Kohatsu had
arrived in Washington, they urged the Justice Department to
detain him for purposes of criminal prosecution pursuant to
18 U.S.C. § 2340A, which authorizes criminal prosecution for acts
of torture committed abroad.[110] No action was taken, however,
while Anderson Kohatsu was in Washington. On March 9, 2000,
Anderson Kohatsu departed Washington and stopped in Houston,
Texas, to change aircraft. As the aircraft prepared to depart,
federal agents boarded and approached Anderson Kohatsu, who
agreed to submit himself for questioning. After several hours of
questioning, the State Department intervened. According to
Undersecretary of State Thomas R. Pickering, Anderson Kohatsu
was entitled to diplomatic immunity and, therefore, he could not be
arrested.[111] As a result, he was allowed to depart on a later flight.
A number of human rights organizations challenged this decision,
arguing that Anderson Kohatsu's visa did not bestow diplomatic
immunity and that the issue of immunity should in any case have
been decided by a court.[112] The Justice Department and some
officials in the State Department reportedly shared the view that
Anderson Kohatsu was not entitled to diplomatic immunity.[113]

Armando Fernández-Larios

On September 11, 1973, the Chilean military overthrew the democratically elected government of Salvador Allende. Following the

---

108 *See* Report No. 54/98, Case 11.756 Leonor La Rosa Bustamente, Inter-American Commission on Human Rights, Dec. 8, 1998. *See* U.S. DEPARTMENT OF STATE, COUNTRY REPORTS ON HUMAN
RIGHTS PRACTICES FOR 1998, at 742 (1999).

109 Anderson Kohatsu was granted a G-2 visa, which is typically issued to foreign government officials conducting business with international organizations in the United States.

110 *See infra* Section 6.

111 DeYoung and Adams, *supra* 105, at A1.

112 Coletta A. Youngers, *The Pinochet Ricochet*, THE NATION, May 8, 2000, at 5.

113 As noted by one Justice Department official, "Our position was he did not. [The State
Department] position was he did. We lost." DeYoung and Adams, *supra* 105, at A1.

coup, military authorities launched a brutal and systematic repression of suspected political opponents. At the time, Winston Cabello worked as an economist for the Allende government and had been appointed the Director of the Regional Planning Office for the Atacama-Coquimbo region in northern Chile. On September 12, 1973, Winston Cabello was detained by local military officials in his home town of Copiapo and accused of subversive activities. He was then imprisoned in the local military garrison.

In a complaint filed in U.S. District Court for the Southern District of Florida, Cabello's family alleges that on or about October 16, 1973, several officers of the Chilean military acting with authorization from General Augusto Pinochet arrived in Copiapo and ordered the elimination of 13 political prisoners being held there.[114] Armando Fernández-Larios was allegedly a member of this group of military officers.[115] He reportedly participated in the torture and execution of Cabello, and helped bring about the executions of the other 12 prisoners.[116] Cabello and the other prisoners were removed from the military garrison and taken to a secluded area. Some of the prisoners were executed immediately; others were slashed with knives before being shot. Although the military claimed that the 13 prisoners had been killed while trying to escape, a Chilean government commission determined after the prisoners' bodies were exhumed that the prisoners had been killed while under the control of the military.[117]

In February 1987, Fernández-Larios entered the United States in connection with an agreement with U.S. officials to provide information concerning the 1976 assassination of former Chilean Ambassador to the United States Orlando Letelier and his assistant Ronni Moffitt.[118]

114 The allegations against Fernández-Larios are based upon the civil complaint filed in U.S. District Court for the Southern District of Florida. See Amended Complaint, Cabello v. Fernández-Larios, Case No. 99-0528-CIV-LENARD (S.D. Fla. 1999).

115 This group and the surrounding atrocities attributed to them have been referred to as the Caravan of Death. See generally David Adams, 27 Years Later, Chile's Caravan of Death Touches U.S., St. Petersburg Times, March 13, 2000, at A1; Steve Anderson, Former Chilean Army Guard Says He Witnessed Executions, U.P.I., June 27, 2000.

116 Amended Complaint, Cabello vs. Fernández-Larios, supra, at 9–10.

117 Id. at 10–12.

118 See generally Douglas Grant Mine, The Assassin Next Door, Part II, Miami New Times, Oct. 12, 2000; Douglas Grant Mine, The Assassin Next Door, Miami New Times, Nov. 18, 1999.

Fernández-Larios subsequently agreed to a plea bargain with U.S. prosecutors and pled guilty to being an "accessory after the fact" in the Letelier bombing. The agreement provided that Fernández-Larios would be placed in the federal Witness Security Program.

Fernández-Larios was later discovered living in the Miami area, and in April 1999, the family of Winston Cabello filed a lawsuit against him pursuant to the Alien Tort Claims Act and the Torture Victim Protection Act. The lawsuit alleges that Fernández-Larios committed acts of summary execution, torture, crimes against humanity, and cruel, inhuman or degrading treatment. The plaintiffs have requested numerous documents from the Chilean government as well as testimony from former Chilean officials.[119] The family's case recently survived motions by Fernández-Larios to dismiss the suit.[120] Trial is anticipated to begin in October 2002.

Emmanuel Constant

In 1993, the Revolutionary Armed Front for the Progress of Haiti ("FRAPH") was established following the coup that removed Haitian president Jean-Bertrand Aristide.[121] Led by Emmanuel "Toto" Constant, FRAPH became the most feared paramilitary group in Haiti. The group is alleged to be responsible for countless killings and acts of torture in 1993 and 1994.[122] In one of the most notorious incidents, Haitian military personnel and members of FRAPH massacred Aristide supporters in the village

119 A Chilean judge investigating the Caravan of Death killings requested the extradition of Fernández-Larios in November 1999. No official response has been issued by the United States government although the Fernández-Larios' plea bargain with federal prosecutors may bar his extradition to Chile. In April 2001, an Argentinian court requested Fernández-Larios' extradition in connection with the assassination in Argentina of former Chilean General Carlos Prats.

120 See Cabello v. Fernández-Larios, 157 F. Supp. 2d 1345 (S.D. Fl. 2001).

121 See generally AMNESTY INTERNATIONAL, HAITI: HUMAN RIGHTS CHALLENGES FACING THE NEW GOVERNMENT (2001); AMNESTY INTERNATIONAL, HAITI: A QUESTION OF JUSTICE (1996); David Grann, Giving the Devil His Due, THE ATLANTIC MONTHLY 55 (June 2001).

122 According to a government truth commission, FRAPH participated in the murder of countless civilians. See generally SI M PA RELE: RAPPORT DE LA COMMISSION NATIONALE DE VERITE ET DE JUSTICE (1997); AMNESTY INTERNATIONAL, HAITI: A QUESTION OF JUSTICE (1996).

of Raboteau in April 1994.[123] As many as 50
people were reported killed.[124]

In December 1994, Constant fled Haiti after
failing to answer a summons issued against him
in connection with a judicial investigation into
FRAPH's involvement in human rights abuses.[125]
He soon arrived in the United States and
settled in New York. After the Haitian government protested his presence in the United
States, Secretary of State Warren Christopher
wrote a letter to Attorney General Janet Reno
urging Constant's deportation to Haiti on
grounds that his continued presence "would
compromise a compelling United States foreign
policy interest."[126] In May 1995, Constant was
arrested by INS officials and found deportable.[127]
He was released by the agency in June 1996, subject to
several conditions, including that he cannot leave the
New York City area and must regularly report to the
INS.[128] Constant stated publicly while in detention that
he had been on the payroll of the CIA at the time of
the military government in Haiti. He was reportedly
released as a result of a secret deal with U.S. authorities in which he agreed to drop a civil suit he had been intending
to bring against them for "wrongful incarceration."[129]

On September 29, 2000, a Haitian court began proceedings
against Constant and 57 other Haitian military and paramilitary

Emmanuel Constant, who
once led the Revolutionary
Armed Front for the Progress
of Haiti, a paramilitary group
alleged to have tortured
and murdered civilians,
at a press conference on
September 22, 1994.

123 *Residents Flee Haitian Town After Killing*, NEW YORK TIMES, Apr. 27, 1994, at A7; *Haitian
Massacre Reported*, CHICAGO TRIBUNE, Apr. 26, 1994, at 3.

124 AMNESTY INTERNATIONAL, ON THE HORNS OF A DILEMMA: MILITARY REPRESSION OR FOREIGN
INVASION? (1994).

125 AMNESTY INTERNATIONAL, ANNUAL REPORT (1996).

126 William Branigin, *Foe of Aristide Now a 'Detainee' in Maryland Jail: Haitian Paramilitary's
Ex-Leader Feels Betrayed by U.S. Officials*, THE WASHINGTON POST, October 27, 1995, in A3.

127 See Marsha Myers, *U.S. Frees Haitian Wanted at Home in Rights Violations*, BALTIMORE SUN,
June 18, 1996, at 7A; Gary Pierre-Pierre, *Haiti Paramilitary Leader is Found Hiding in Queens*,
NEW YORK TIMES, May 13, 1995, at 4.

128 Grann, *supra*, at 68.

129 AMNESTY INTERNATIONAL, ANNUAL REPORT (1997).

Protestors outside the home of Emmanuel Constant on Aug. 9, 1997 carry signs referring to the abuses allegedly committed by a Haitian paramilitary group that Constant once led.

officials based upon their participation in the Raboteau massacre.[130] Although there was no evidence that Constant had personally committed acts of torture or murder, he was accused of being responsible for the actions of individuals under his command. In November 2000, Constant was convicted *in absentia* by a Haitian jury of murder, attempted murder, and torture and sentenced to life imprisonment and hard labor.[131] Under Haitian law, Constant is entitled to a new trial if he returns to Haiti.[132]

Haitian immigrants and human rights organizations have long protested Constant's presence in the United States.[133] Calls for his deportation to Haiti became even more vocal after his November 2000 conviction in the Raboteau massacre trial. The Justice Department has indicated, however, that there are no plans to deport Constant.[134]

130 AMNESTY INTERNATIONAL, HAITI: HUMAN RIGHTS CHALLENGES FACING THE NEW GOVERNMENT (2001).

131 Ron Howell, *Convicted in Haiti, 'Toto' Constant Fears Extradition*, NEWSDAY, Nov. 18, 2000, at A7; *Haiti Court Convicts 16 in '94 Coup Massacre*, NEW YORK TIMES, Nov. 12, 2000, at 18.

132 Amnesty International believes that *in absentia* trials are inconsistent with the right to be tried in one's presence, and would support a new trial before different judges if Constant were returned to Haiti. See *Haiti Junta is Sentenced in Absentia*, NEW YORK TIMES, Nov. 19, 2000, at 15.

133 See Niles Lathem, *CIA Harbors Haitian Killers in Qns.*, NEW YORK POST, May 14, 2001, at 7; Leslie Casimir, *March Targets Haiti Suspect*, DAILY NEWS, Dec. 13, 2000, at 31; Ron Howell, *Haunted by Haitian Violence: Queens Man, Target of Protests, Responds to Accusations of Terror*, NEWSDAY, Sept. 5, 2000, at A4; Amy Waldman, *Haitians Cry 'Assassin' Outside Queens Home*, NEW YORK TIMES, Aug. 13, 2000, at A29; Sarah Kershaw, *Renewed Outcry on Haitian Fugitive in Queens*, NEW YORK TIMES, Aug. 12, 2000, at B2.

134 Ron Howell, *Convicted in Haiti, 'Toto' Constant Fears Extradition*, NEWSDAY, Nov. 18, 2000, at A7.

*****

Like the individuals described in the preceding case studies, the following individuals are alleged in judicial proceedings to be responsible for human rights abuses in their countries of origin. They also managed to enter and, in some cases, establish residence in, the United States. Some entered lawfully and overstayed their visas. Others entered through misrepresentation or without proper documentation. And some entered with the approval or assistance of the U.S. Government. Each case further demonstrates the need for a consistent and multi-tiered policy for bringing alleged human rights abusers to justice.

Alvaro Rafael Saravia Marino

Former Salvadoran Army captain Alvaro Rafael Saravia Marino is a key suspect in the 1980 assassination of Monsignor Oscar Romero, Archbishop of El Salvador.[135] In 1988, Saravia was arrested in Miami, Florida, after the Attorney General of El Salvador sought to have him extradited from the United States for his alleged role in the assassination. The U.S. District Court for the Southern District of Florida granted the request, finding probable cause to believe that Romero's death was accomplished by a premeditated plan to assassinate him and that Saravia was a "knowing, active participant in the execution of that plan." However, Saravia was released by the District Court after the Supreme Court of El Salvador invalidated the extradition demand.[136]

Archbishop Romero's assassination was investigated by a United Nations-sponsored Truth Commission, which in 1993 concluded that Saravia was actively involved in planning and

135 Archbishop Romero, an outspoken critic of human rights violations in El Salvador, was shot and killed on March 24, 1980. Earlier that month, he had written to then President Jimmy Carter, urging the United States to stop providing the military training and equipment that was being used to commit human rights violations in El Salvador. AMNESTY INTERNATIONAL, EL SALVADOR: PEACE CAN ONLY BE ACHIEVED WITH JUSTICE (April 2001). Declassified State Department and CIA documents reveal that the United States Government was aware of Saravia's involvement in the assassination as early as May 1980. Lauren Gilbert, *El Salvador's Death Squads: New Evidence from U.S. Documents*, The Center for International Policy (March 1994); JAMES R. BROCKMAN, ROMERO: A LIFE 249 (1989).

136 In Re Extradition of Alvaro Rafael Saravia, Case No. 8703598-CIV-EXTRADITION-JOHNSON, United States District Court, Southern District of Florida (September 27, 1988).

Col. Carl Dorelien, who was convicted *in absentia* in Haiti of involvement in a 1994 massacre in the village of Raboteau, at army head-quarters in Port-Au-Prince, Haiti, on Oct. 18, 1993.

carrying out the assassination.[137] The Commission also concluded that the Supreme Court of El Salvador had played an active role in preventing the extradition of Saravia from the United States, thus ensuring impunity for the other high-ranking military officers involved in the assassination.

Saravia has reportedly been living in the United States since 1985 and may have applied for political asylum.[138]

Carl Dorelien

Haitian Army Colonel Carl Dorelien was head of personnel in the *de facto* military government that replaced the democratically elected government of President Jean-Bertrand Aristide following a violent coup in 1991. From 1991 to 1994, the Haitian Armed Forces and its allies were responsible for widespread human rights violations; civilians suspected of supporting Aristide were beaten, imprisoned, or killed. The village of Raboteau was specifically targeted for repression because of the strong support of its inhabitants for Aristide. In April 1994, as many as 50 people were killed after they were surrounded and attacked by military and paramilitary forces. Homes were sacked and burned. Many people died from beatings or from gunshots while others drowned as they fled into the sea.[139]

Following Haiti's return to constitutional order in October 1994, Dorelien emigrated to the United States, reportedly with the

---

137 UNITED NATIONS COMMISSION ON THE TRUTH FOR EL SALVADOR, FROM MADNESS TO HOPE: THE 12-YEAR WAR IN EL SALVADOR 131 (1993). In April 2000, the Inter-American Commission on Human Rights concluded that Saravia was involved in the planning of the assassination and paid the assassins. *See* Inter-American Commission on Human Rights, Report No. 37/00, Case 11481 (April 13, 2000).

138 Alfonso Chardy, *Scores Accused of Atrocities Committed in Other Countries Are Quietly Living in U.S.*, MIAMI HERALD, July 22, 2001.

139 AMNESTY INTERNATIONAL, HAITI: STEPS FORWARD, STEPS BACK: 10 YEARS AFTER THE COUP (2001).

assistance of the U.S. Government.[140] In June 1997, while living in Florida, he won $3.2 million in the state lottery. In February 1998, a warrant was issued in Haiti for Dorelien's arrest on account of his alleged role in masterminding the Raboteau massacre. In November 2000, he was tried and convicted *in absentia* in Haiti of premeditated, voluntary homicide and sentenced to life imprisonment.[141] In June 2001, Dorelien was arrested by the INS and is now in deportation proceedings.[142]

Donaldo Alvarez Ruíz

Donaldo Alvarez Ruíz served as Minister of the Interior in Guatemala under the 1978–82 government of General Romeo Lucas García. Testimony contained in the 1999 report of the United Nations-sponsored Historical Clarification Commission alleges that Alvarez personally supervised the work of death squads, which were responsible for the "disappearance," torture, and execution of thousands of Guatemalan citizens.[143] Judicial proceedings have been initiated against Alvarez in two prominent cases. In December 1999, indigenous leader and Nobel Prize laureate Rigoberta Menchú lodged a suit in the Spanish National Court accusing Alvarez and seven former officials of genocide, torture, murder, terrorism, and illegal arrest.[144] In December 2000, the Spanish National Court ruled that it did not currently have juris-

140 Steve Fainaru, *INS Moves to Track Down Rights Abusers,* BOSTON GLOBE, Sept. 20, 1999, at A1; Del Quentin Wilber, *Rights Abusers Can Find Haven: U.S. Immigration Law Enables Torturers to Enter, Stay Safely,* THE BALTIMORE SUN, Aug. 28, 2000.

141 Rin Howell, *Convicted in Haiti, 'Toto' Constant Fears Extradition,* NEWSDAY, Nov. 18, 2000, at A7. When he returns to Haiti, Dorelien is entitled to a new trial. Amnesty International believes that *in absentia* trials are inconsistent with the right to be tried in one's presence and would support a new trial before different judges if Dorelien were returned to Haiti.

142 Colleen Mastony, *INS Arrests Port St. Lucie Man Tied to '94 Slayings in Haiti,* PALM BEACH POST, June 23, 2001, at 1B.

143 UNITED NATIONS COMMISSION FOR HISTORICAL CLARIFICATION, GUATEMALA: MEMORY OF SILENCE (February 25, 1999).

144 The Rigoberta Menchú Foundation has appealed against the ruling before Spain's Supreme Court. See Menchú Case: Spanish High Court Summons Witnesses 4/19/00, Guatemalan Human Rights Commission/USA, Update #8/00, April 30, 2000; Nefer Munoz, *Rights-Guatemala: Activists Berate Spain's Prosecutor's Office,* INTER PRESS SERVICE, December 4, 2000; AMNESTY INTERNATIONAL, SPAIN/GUATEMALA: UNIVERSAL JURISDICTION SHOULD APPLY TO CRIMES AGAINST HUMANITY (December 2000).

diction to hear the case. Alvarez also faces criminal charges in Guatemala stemming from the case of two girls and an infant who were "disappeared" during a counterinsurgency operation in 1981.[145]

Alvarez reportedly resided in the United States until recently and is since known to have made frequent visits to the United States.

Juan Alesio Samayoa

Former Guatemalan military commissioner and civil patrol leader Juan Alesio Samayoa is accused by indigenous inhabitants of the Tululché estate in El Quiché of having committed or ordered over 150 human rights abuses in the early 1980s. During the long-term civil conflict in Guatemala, military commissioners were often in charge of organizing "civil defense patrols," which acted at the behest of the military. In the early 1980s, the local civil defense patrol at the Tululché estate reportedly terrorized and subjected the Quiché-speaking villagers to torture, rape, kidnapping, and murder in order to obtain the villagers' land.[146]

In 1992, surviving victims and witnesses of the Tululché massacres initiated proceedings in a Guatemalan court against Alesio and five others, including Alesio's former fellow commissioner and alleged accomplice, Cándido Noriega Estrada. Alesio and Noriega were charged with 35 murders, 44 kidnappings, 14 rapes, and 53 other attacks on individuals, including torture.[147] Alesio took refuge in a military hospital when his arrest was ordered and was allegedly flown by the Guatemalan military to the United States, where he reportedly remains.[148]

---

145 *Case of Disappeared Children Presented to Authorities,* Cerigua Weekly Briefs, August 6, 1998; AMNESTY INTERNATIONAL, GUATEMALA: 'DISAPPEARANCES' BRIEFING TO THE UN COMMITTEE AGAINST TORTURE (November 30, 2000).

146 *See* AMNESTY INTERNATIONAL, RACISM AND THE ADMINISTRATION OF JUSTICE (July 2001).

147 Amnesty International Urgent Action Appeal, *Guatemala: Witnesses in the Tululché Trial; Rolando Colindres, lawyer; Lucrecia Barreintos, lawyer; and Juan Jeremias Tecu, CONFREGUA* (May 21, 1999).

148 AMNESTY INTERNATIONAL, GUATEMALA'S LETHAL LEGACY: PAST IMPUNITY AND RENEWED HUMAN RIGHTS VIOLATIONS (February 2002).

In November 1999, Cándido Noriega Estrada, who is Alesio's codefendant in the Tululché trial, was convicted of six first degree murders and two homicides and sentenced to 220 years in prison by the Sentencing Tribunal of Tontonicapán.[149] The case against Alesio remains open and a warrant has been issued for his arrest.[150]

Eriberto Mederos

Eriberto Mederos is a former hospital orderly accused of torture by political prisoners who were confined to wards run by Cuban state security in Havana's National Psychiatric Hospital during the 1970s.[151] Mederos has claimed that he was following doctors' orders when he administered electroshock to patients, who had not been anesthetized, on a bare floor covered with the patients' urine and excrement.[152] In 1993, Mederos became a naturalized U.S. citizen.[153] He has reportedly received two state nursing licenses.[154]

In April 23, 2001, U.S. Representatives Ileana Ros-Lehtinen and Lincoln Diaz-Balart called on the U.S. Department of Justice to review

149 The verdict was upheld on appeal in February 2000 and the Supreme Court of Guatemala confirmed the sentence in August 2000. This was Noriega's third trial stemming from the proceedings the Tululché villagers initiated against him in 1992. In 1997, he was acquitted of all charges in a trial that the United Nations Verification Mission in Guatemala found marred by grave violations of due process and clear institutional deficiencies: the indigenous witnesses complained of inadequate translation arrangements, bias on the part of the court, and repeated intimidation by Noriega, his family, and followers. A second trial in April 1999, which an Amnesty International trial observer reported was also marked by bias on the part of court officials, found Noriega not guilty for a selected sample of the best-documented abuses of which he was originally accused. *See* AMNESTY INTERNATIONAL, A DOUBLE-EDGED SWORD—GUATEMALAN COURT SENDS NOTORIOUS HUMAN RIGHTS CASE TO RETRIAL (JULY 1999); U.S. DEP'T OF STATE, BUREAU OF DEMOCRACY, HUMAN RIGHTS, AND LABOR, 1999 COUNTRY REPORTS ON HUMAN RIGHTS PRACTICES: GUATEMALA (2000).

150 U.S. DEP'T OF STATE, BUREAU OF DEMOCRACY, HUMAN RIGHTS, AND LABOR, 2000 COUNTRY REPORTS ON HUMAN RIGHTS PRACTICES: GUATEMALA (2001).

151 *See generally,* John-Thor Dahlburg, *Alleged Torturer Now a U.S. Citizen,* LOS ANGELES TIMES, Nov. 11, 2001, at A37; Pablo Alfonso, *Accused Cuban Torturer On Hialeah Nursing Staff,* MIAMI HERALD, April 16, 1992, at A1.

152 Mederos claimed that the treatment was not administered with the intent to torture. Alfonso, *supra,* at A1.

153 Niles Lathem, *War-Crime Fiends Flock to U.S.,* NEW YORK POST, May 14, 2001, at 6; Jody A. Benjamin, *Patients Detail Case against Nurse: 2 Legislators Seek Revocation of U.S. Citizenship,* SUN-SENTINEL, Apr. 24, 2001, at 3B; Alfonso Chardy, *Nazi Hunter on Quest to Expel Other 'Torturers,'* MIAMI HERALD, March 12, 2001, at A1.

154 The Florida Department of Health, *Health Licensee and Continuing Education Providers Information* (http://www.doh.state.fl.us). *See also* Chitra Ragavan, *A Tale Of Torture and Intrigue,* U.S. NEWS & WORLD REPORT, September 10, 2001. *See generally* Charles J. Brown and Armando Lago, *The Politics of Psychiatry in Revolutionary Cuba* (1991).

Gen. Luis Alonso Discua Elvir, the former commander-in-chief of the Honduran armed forces who once led a covert military intelligence unit responsible for human rights abuses, at an armed forces commander's hand over ceremony on December 21, 1995.

evidence that reportedly supports the allegations against Mederos and to consider revoking his citizenship or prosecuting him.[155] On September 4, 2001, INS officials arrested Mederos after a federal grand jury indicted him on charges of fraudulently obtaining U.S. citizenship by denying that he had ever persecuted anyone.[156]

Luis Alonso Discua Elvir, Juan Angel Hernandez Lara, and Juan Evangelista López Grijalba

Luis Alonso Discua Elvir and Juan Angel Hernandez Lara are former Honduran military officers reportedly linked to Battalion 3-16, a covert military intelligence unit responsible for the abduction, detention, torture, and murder of political suspects in Honduras in the 1980s.[157] Discua Elvir, the former head of the Honduran armed forces who once commanded Battalion 3-16, is among the senior political and military figures linked by the National Commissioner for the Protection of Human Rights in Honduras to the "systematic, clandestine and organized" practice of "disappearance" against political opponents throughout the 1980s.[158]

155 Alfonso Chardy, *Lawmakers Ask Deportation Of Cuban 'Torturer' From U.S.*, MIAMI HERALD, April 24, 2001.

156 If convicted, Mederos faces up to five years in a federal prison and $250,000 in fines, and could be stripped of his United States citizenship. *See "Alleged Cuban Torturer Arrested in Miami,"* Reuters, September 5, 2001.

157 Declassified documents and other sources have shown that Battalion 3-16 was trained, equipped, and supported by the CIA, which was, along with the United States Embassy, aware of the human rights violations for which Battalion 3-16 was responsible and even participated in some interrogations. *See* Alec Dubro and Martha Honey, *UN Ambassador John Negroponte,* 5 THE PROGRESSIVE RESPONSE, March 23, 2001; Gary Cohn and Ginger Thompson, *Unearthed: Fatal Secrets,* BALTIMORE SUN, June 11, 1995; Alfonso Chardy, *Alleged Death Squad Returns to Spotlight,* MIAMI HERALD, April 16, 2001; AMNESTY INTERNATIONAL, HONDURAS: THE BEGINNING OF THE END OF IMPUNITY? (1995); AMNESTY INTERNATIONAL, HONDURAS: CIVILIAN AUTHORITY, MILITARY POWER, AND HUMAN RIGHTS VIOLATIONS IN THE 1980s (1988).

158 HUMAN RIGHTS WATCH, THE FACTS SPEAK FOR THEMSELVES: THE PRELIMINARY REPORT ON DISAPPEARANCES OF THE NATIONAL COMMISSIONER FOR THE PROTECTION OF HUMAN RIGHTS IN HONDURAS 151, 152, 238 (1994); AMNESTY INTERNATIONAL, HONDURAS: THE BEGINNING OF THE END OF IMPUNITY? (1995).

Hernandez Lara is a former officer in the Honduran armed forces who, according to the INS, admitted to "kicking, punching, placing pins under the fingernails and plastic bags on the heads of four victims who were later killed."[159]

Discua Elvir and Hernandez Lara were deported from the United States in the early months of 2001, just weeks before John Negroponte, the former U.S. Ambassador to Honduras accused of covering up the human rights abuses committed by the unit, was nominated to be U.S. Ambassador to the United Nations.[160]

A third officer with links to the unit, Juan Evangelista López Grijalba, was reportedly granted temporary protected status by the State Department.[161] López Grijalba is the former head of the G-2, the intelligence division of the General Staff of the Honduran armed forces, and one of ten military officers charged by the Special Prosecutor for Human Rights in Honduras with the attempted murder and unlawful detention of six university students in 1982.[162]

Yusuf Abdi Ali

Yusuf Abdi Ali served as a colonel in the Somali military under the government of Major-General Mohamed Siad Barre.[163] From 1969–1991, military, security, and political officials in the Siad Barre

159 Alfonso Chardy, *Alleged Death Squad Returns to Spotlight*, MIAMI HERALD, April 16, 2001.
160 A staff member in the U.S. Embassy who served under the Ambassador claims that he was ordered to remove all mention of torture and executions from the draft of his 1982 report on the human rights situation in Honduras. *See* Alec Dubro and Martha Honey, *UN Ambassador John Negroponte*, 5 THE PROGRESSIVE RESPONSE, March 23, 2001; Gary Cohn and Ginger Thompson, *Unearthed: Fatal Secrets*, BALTIMORE SUN, June 11, 1995. The State Department reportedly cancelled Discua's diplomatic visa on February 28, 2001. Hernandez Lara was reportedly arrested by the INS on June 16,2000 and deported to Honduras on January 17, 2001. He was arrested again on March 28, 2001 after reentering the United States and is reported to be in a Miami detention center pending trial for illegal reentry after deportation. *See* T. Christian Miller and Maggie Farley, *Timing of Envoy's Deportation Raises Question*, LOS ANGELES TIMES, May 7, 2001; *Negroponte Witness Deported*, Weekly News Update on the Americas, Nicaragua Solidarity Network of Greater New York (http://www.americas.org).
161 Joseph Contreras, *Found: A Foreign Fugitive*, NEWSWEEK, April 19, 2001; Joseph Contreras, *Looking for the Bad Guys*, NEWSWEEK, April 16, 2001.
162 AMNESTY INTERNATIONAL, HONDURAS: CONTINUED STRUGGLE AGAINST IMPUNITY (1996). *See also* HUMAN RIGHTS WATCH, THE FACTS SPEAK FOR THEMSELVES: THE PRELIMINARY REPORT ON DISAPPEARANCES OF THE NATIONAL COMMISSIONER FOR THE PROTECTION OF HUMAN RIGHTS IN HONDURAS 136-138 (1994).
163 *See* Mary Williams Walsh, *Canada Said to Be a Haven for Somali War Criminals*, LOS ANGELES TIMES, October 7, 1992. *See also* Greg Quill, *CBC tracks war criminals African 'murderers and torturers' in Canada*, THE TORONTO STAR, October 6, 1992, at E1. *See generally* AMNESTY INTERNATIONAL, SOMALIA: BUILDING HUMAN RIGHTS IN THE DISINTEGRATED STATE (1995).

Gen. Prosper Avril, who ruled Haiti from 1988 until he was ousted in 1990, speaks at an April 1989 news conference. In 1994, a U.S. court ordered Avril to pay $41 million in damages to six Haitians who brought a lawsuit against him under the Alien Tort Claims Act.

government were responsible for, or personally carried out, massive human rights violations, including the routine torture of political prisoners, thousands of detentions without charge or trial, grossly unfair political trials, many of which resulted in executions, and extrajudicial executions of thousands of civilians.

After the Siad Barre government was overthrown in 1991, Ali sought asylum in Canada. In 1992, he was deported to the United States, after the Canadian Broadcasting Corporation aired "Crimes Against Humanity," a documentary that presented witness testimony alleging that Ali ordered the execution of more than 100 people in Somalia. Ali, who is reported to have originally come to the United States from Somalia on a diplomatic visa in 1990, eventually settled in Virginia.[164] In 1998, the INS arrested Ali, alleging that he was directly involved in incidents that led to the deaths of thousands of people.[165] The agency sought to have Ali deported on grounds that he had committed fraud by denying on immigration documents that he had ever participated in genocidal acts. The case was dismissed, reportedly because Ali had already withdrawn his application for residency status.

*****

More than 70 lawsuits have been filed in U.S. courts against persons who are alleged to be responsible for torture or other grave

164 Ali was reportedly granted a visa by the U.S. Government so that he could receive counter-insurgency and armed combat training at Fort Leavenworth, Kansas. *See The Accused: Safe Haven in US for an Alleged Somali War Criminal*, CBS NEWS TRANSCRIPTS, June 25, 1993; Jack Lackey, *Ex-Leader of Somali Forces Deported*, THE TORONTO STAR, October 10, 1992, at A17.

165 U.S. government officials claim that Ali was expelled from the United States after being deported from Canada in 1992, but that he later reentered the United States after giving misleading information. *See* David Stout, Ex-Somali Officer is Arrested in Virginia, THE NEW YORK TIMES, February 28, 1998; Steve Fainaru, Rights Violators Exploit US Immigration System, BOSTON GLOBE, May 4,1999, at A1; Chitra Ragavan, *A Safe Haven, But for Whom?*, U.S. NEWS & WORLD REP., Nov. 15, 1999, at 22.

human rights abuses in other countries and who were found to be living in, or visiting, the United States.[166] In addition to the lawsuits filed against Kelbessa Negewo, Nikola Vukovic, and Armando Fernández-Larios, lawsuits have also been filed against the following individuals who once resided, or continue to reside, in the United States.

Prosper Avril

Former Haitian General Prosper Avril served as chief of presidential security under President Jean-Claude Duvalier in Haiti, until the latter was ousted from power in February 1986. In 1988, Avril became *de facto* president of Haiti following a coup d'état. Under Avril's leadership, reports of torture and ill-treatment of political and common-law prisoners became widespread. In March 1990, in the face of mounting domestic and international pressure, Avril went into exile in the United States.

In 1991, six Haitian opposition leaders represented by the Center for Constitutional Rights filed a lawsuit against Avril in U.S. District Court for the Southern District of Florida. The suit alleged that Avril issued orders for the six men to be detained and tortured. In 1994, the District Court found that Avril, who had returned to Haiti in 1992, "bears personal responsibility for a systematic pattern of egregious human rights abuses in Haiti during his military rule of September 1988 until March 1990. He also bears personal responsibility for the interrogation and torture of each of the plaintiffs in this case."[167] The plaintiffs were awarded $41 million in damages.

On May 26, 2001, Avril was arrested in Haiti, pursuant to a warrant issued in 1996 that accused Avril of the illegal arrest, assault, and torture of the six Haitian activists who brought the lawsuit against him in Florida.[168]

---

166 For an elaboration of civil lawsuits brought against suspected torturers, see Section 6 *infra.*

167 Paul v. Avril, 901 F. Supp. 330, 335 (S.D. Fla 1984).

168 Judicial authorities in Haiti are in the process of determining the parameters of the case against Avril. *See generally* AMNESTY INTERNATIONAL, HAITI: ONE MORE STEP TOWARDS THE END OF IMPUNITY (June 6, 2001).

AP/Wide World Photos

Gen. Héctor Alejandro Gramajo Morales, former Minister of Defense of Guatemala. In 1995, a U.S. court ordered Gramajo to pay $47.5 million to eight Guatemalans and an American who brought a lawsuit against him under the Torture Victim Protection Act and Alien Tort Claims Act.

Héctor Alejandro Gramajo Morales

General Héctor Alejandro Gramajo Morales, a graduate of the School of the Americas in Fort Benning, Georgia, was head of the Guatemalan Army High Command before becoming Minister of Defense during the 1980s.[169] He has admitted to having played a key role in the planning and implementation of the counter-insurgency strategy that led to a well-documented pattern of gross abuses in Guatemala in the 1980s, including the massacre of entire villages.[170] In 1991, Gramajo received a degree in public administration from the John F. Kennedy School of Government at Harvard University, which he reportedly attended with the assistance of the U.S. Agency for International Development.[171]

In April 1995, the U.S. District Court for the District of Massachusetts, found Gramajo bore command responsibility for a campaign of systematic human rights violations in Guatemala in which tens of thousands were murdered, tortured, and

169 The School of the Americas is a United States military training facility for foreign officers. In September 1996 the United States Department of Defense released evidence that the School of Americas had used so-called "intelligence training manuals" between 1982 and 1991 that advocated execution, torture, beatings, and blackmail. The manuals were used to train thousands of Latin American security force agents in Colombia, Ecuador, El Salvador, Guatemala, and Peru. See AMNESTY INTERNATIONAL, STOPPING THE TORTURE TRADE (1995). Other School of the Americas graduates mentioned in this report include: Roberto D'Aubuisson, Luis Alonso Discua Elvir, Juan Evangelista Lopez Grijalva, and José Guillermo García; Carlos Eugenio Vides Casanova was a guest speaker. See School of the Americas Watch, http://www.soaw.org/soag.html. The School of the Americas was replaced by the Western Hemisphere Institute for Security Cooperation in January 2001.

170 AMNESTY INTERNATIONAL, PRESIDENTIAL CANDIDATE GENERAL HÉCTOR GRAMAJO HELD RESPONSIBLE FOR GROSS HUMAN RIGHTS VIOLATIONS BY UNITED STATES FEDERAL COURT (1995).

171 See Anthony Flint, Guatemalan General Given Lawsuit at Harvard, BOSTON GLOBE, June 6, 1991, at 22; Alexander Cockburn, Harvard's New Policy on Murder, THE NATION, May 1, 1995. "Statement of Sister Dianna Ortiz on the Report of the Intelligence Oversight Board," Guatemala Human Rights Commission, July 1, 1996.

"disappeared."[172] He was ordered to pay $47.5 million in damages to the plaintiffs, including an American citizen who was raped and tortured by military and security force personnel, and eight Guatemalan survivors and witnesses of human rights abuses carried out by soldiers acting under Gramajo's command.

Sintong Panjaitan

On November 12, 1991, Indonesian government troops opened fire on a peaceful demonstration at the Santa Cruz cemetery in Dili. Over 270 people were killed. The victims were among some 2,000 people who had joined a procession to the cemetery for Sebastiao Gomes, who was reportedly killed by Indonesian security forces on October 28, 1991. After the massacre, the bodies of the dead were loaded onto military trucks and buried either in unmarked graves or at sea.[173]

In August 1992, Helen Todd, the mother of Kamal Bamadhaj, a New Zealander killed during the massacre, filed a lawsuit against retired Indonesian General Sintong Panjaitan in U.S. District Court for the District of Massachusetts.[174] The suit alleged that Panjaitan bore responsibility for the massacre, which was carried out by troops under his command. Panjaitan, who was relieved of his post after the massacre, had been living in Boston, ostensibly to attend Harvard University. He returned to Indonesia shortly after the lawsuit was filed and did not appear at the trial.[175] In October 1994, the court granted a default judgment for the plaintiffs when Panjaitan failed to present a defense. Damages were set at $14 million.

172 Gramajo failed to defend the suit and was found guilty by default. The court concluded that plaintiffs had "demonstrated that, at a minimum, Gramajo was aware of and supported widespread acts of brutality committed by personnel under his command resulting in thousands of civilian deaths." The judgment was made in response to two lawsuits brought by the Center for Constitutional Rights in 1991: Xuncax v. Gramajo, 886 F. Supp. 162 (D. Mass. 1995). See generally AMNESTY INTERNATIONAL, PRESIDENTIAL CANDIDATE GENERAL HÉCTOR GRAMAJO HELD RESPONSIBLE FOR GROSS HUMAN RIGHTS VIOLATIONS BY UNITED STATES FEDERAL COURT (April 1995).

173 AMNESTY INTERNATIONAL, POWER AND IMPUNITY: HUMAN RIGHTS UNDER THE NEW ORDER (1994).

174 Todd v. Panjaitan, Civ. A. No. 92-12255-PBS, 1994 WI 827111 (D. Mass. Oct. 26, 1994); Michael Ellis, US Court Rules $14 Million Against Indonesian General, REUTERS, October 27, 1994.

175 Indonesian Sued For East Timor Massacre, REUTERS, October 24, 1994.

Gen. José Guillermo García, former Minister of Defense of El Salvador, at a military procession in 1981. Garcia is named in two lawsuits brought in U.S. courts under the Torture Victim Protection Act and Alien Tort Claims Act.

Carlos Eugenio Vides Casanova and José Guillermo García

In May 1999, the Center for Justice & Accountability filed a civil suit in U.S. District Court for the Southern District of Florida against General Carlos Eugenio Vides Casanova (the Director-General of the Salvadoran National Guard from 1979–1983 who then became Minister of Defense) and General José Guillermo García (Minister of Defense from 1979–1983), both of whom had moved to the United States in 1989.[176] The lawsuit alleges that Vides Casanova and García exercised command responsibility over members of the Salvadoran military and security forces who committed torture, crimes against humanity, acts of cruel, inhuman and degrading treatment, and arbitrary detention.[177]

The plaintiffs are three Salvadorans: a doctor who was allegedly abducted, detained, and tortured by the Salvadoran National Guard in late 1980 in the Guard's national headquarters; a Church layworker who was allegedly abducted, detained, tortured, and raped by National Guardsmen in late 1979; and a professor at the University of El Salvador who was allegedly dragged from his classroom, detained, and tortured by the National Police in their national headquarters in 1983. A trial date remains pending.

The Lawyers Committee for Human Rights helped bring a similar case against the same two generals on behalf of the families of

176 García is reported to have received political asylum. Vides Casanova was granted legal permanent residency. See Susan Spencer-Wendel, *Salvadoran Generals Face Jury in Nun Slayings*, THE PALM BEACH POST, October 1, 2000; Karen Meadows, *Salvadoran Murders Revisited*, THE ASSOCIATED PRESS, November 2, 2000; *Churchwomen's Case Goes to Trial*, Central America/Mexico Report, Religious Task Force on Central America and Mexico, September 2000; Yolanda Chávez Leyva, *U.S. Must Take Responsibility for Aiding El Salvador Murderers*, THE PROGRESSIVE MEDIA PROJECT, November 21, 2000.

177 The allegations against Garcia and Vides Casanova are contained in a civil complaint filed with the U.S. District Court for the Southern District of Florida, Romagoza et al v. Vides Casanova and García, S.D. Fla. 99-8364-CIV-HURLEY.

four American women who were
allegedly abducted, raped, and murdered by the Salvadoran National
Guard in 1980.[178] A jury heard that case
in October 2000 and rendered a verdict
that the generals were not liable for
the crimes, reportedly on the premise
that they did not have "effective
control" over their subordinates.[179] The
case is now on appeal before the
Eleventh Circuit Court of Appeals.

In 1993, the United Nations-
sponsored Truth Commission in El
Salvador concluded that Vides
Casanova concealed the fact that the
murders had been carried out pursuant
to superior orders and that García
made no serious effort to investigate those responsible for the murders.[180] Robert E. White, former U.S.
Ambassador to El Salvador, has testified that the
failure of García, Vides Casanova, and other members
of the Salvadoran military high command to take
serious action to investigate and prosecute human
rights abuses by their personnel led to the deaths of thousands,
including the American women.[181]

Gen. Carlos Eugenio Vides
Casanova, former Director-
General of the Salvadoran
National Guard, is named in
two lawsuits brought in U.S.
courts under the Torture
Victim Protection Act and
Alien Tort Claims Act.

178 Ford et al v. Vides Casanova and Garcia, S.D. Fla. 99-8359-CIV-HURLEY. In March 1998, four
of the five Guardsmen who had been convicted of the crime in El Salvador in May 1984 admitted
that they acted on orders of higher-level officials. See Lawyers Committee for Human Rights,
Former Salvadoran Officials Face U.S. Law Suit For Role In American Churchwomen Murders
(1999); Lawyers Committee for Human Rights, *Briefing on the Search for Full Disclosure of the
Circumstances Which Led to the Death of Four U.S. Churchwomen in El Salvador in 1980* (1998).

179 See generally Sean D. Murphy, Acquittal of Salvadoran Generals in Nuns' Death, 95 AM. J.
INT'L L. 394 (2001); Elinor J. Brecher, Jury Clears Two Salvadoran Ex-Generals in Deaths of U.S.
Churchwomen, MIAMI HERALD, Nov. 4, 2000; David Gonzalez, 2 Salvadoran Generals Cleared by
U.S. Jury in Nuns' Deaths, NEW YORK TIMES, Nov. 4, 2000.

180 UNITED NATIONS COMMISSION ON THE TRUTH FOR EL SALVADOR, FROM MADNESS TO HOPE: THE
12-YEAR WAR IN EL SALVADOR 62 (1993).

181 Declassified telegrams describe the efforts of former United States Ambassador to El
Salvador Robert E. White's efforts to convince Garcia and Vides Casanova to put an end to
military death squads. See Robert E. White, *Justice Denied*, COMMONWEAL, December 1, 2000.

6: U.S. policy towards torture

*"If Toto Constant himself can circulate in New York
without worry, then how can I, as a victim, circulate
without worry?"*
—Alerte Belance[182]
Torture survivor from Haiti

U.S. policy towards torture has long exhibited a paradox of values.
On the one hand, the United States has regularly condemned
torture and has been a firm supporter of international efforts
to prohibit and punish torture. It was a leader in efforts to
establish the International Covenant on Civil and Political Rights
and the Convention against Torture. It recently instituted procedures to implement the provisions of the Convention against
Torture with respect to the rule of *non-refoulement.* It has
established procedures for torture victims to seek civil remedies
against perpetrators. It has imposed criminal penalties for acts
of extraterritorial torture. It has also provided financial contributions to national and international programs that assist
torture victims.

On the other hand, the United States has not fully implemented its obligations under the Convention against Torture.
While the United States supported the adoption of the Convention against Torture in 1984, the U.S. Senate did not provide
its advice and consent until 1990, and the United States did not
ratify the treaty until 1994. Moreover, the United States attached
a series of reservations, understandings, and declarations to its
instrument of ratification that purport to limit the application of
the Convention against Torture.[183] While the United States has
gradually adopted legislation to implement the Convention

---

182 *See supra* Section 5.

183 The Committee against Torture has recommended that the United States withdraw its
reservations, interpretations, and understandings relating to the Convention against Torture.
See U.N. Press Release on Committee against Torture, 24th Sess. (May 15, 2000); Sean Murphy,
UN Reaction to Torture Report, 94 AM. J. INT'L L. 528 (2000). *See generally* Louis Henkin, *U.S.
Ratification of Human Rights Conventions: The Ghost of Senator Bricker,* 89 AM. J. INT'L L. 341
(1993).

49

against Torture, some of these provisions remain unenforced. In particular, the United States has yet to seek criminal prosecution of suspected torturers located in the United States.

The failure of the United States to prosecute suspected torturers has been made more conspicuous by what appears to be a preference for using immigration law in lieu of criminal law to deal with alleged perpetrators. In November 2000, for example, the INS began detaining for the purpose of deportation aliens who allegedly committed human rights abuses in foreign countries.[184] At the same time, Congress began debating extending immigration restrictions to aliens who have committed human rights violations.[185] While these efforts may be motivated by the desire to ensure the United States does not become a safe haven for torturers, they are not an acceptable substitute for extradition or prosecution, which the U.S. Government is obliged to pursue as a party to the Convention against Torture.

The following sections examine four mechanisms for challenging impunity in the United States: (A) extradition and surrender proceedings; (B) criminal prosecution; (C) civil litigation; and (D) immigration restrictions.

Extradition and surrender proceedings

Extradition provides one mechanism by which the United States can fulfill its obligation to ensure that those responsible for torture are brought to justice.[186] The obligation to extradite suspected torturers is expressly set forth in the Convention against Torture. It is an obligation the United States also recognizes in its own extradition agreements.[187]

---

184 *See* Noreen Marcus, *INS Arrests 7 Suspected Rights Violators*, SUN-SENTINEL, May 9, 2001, at 7B; Jody A. Benjamin, *INS Arrests 14 in Rights Abuses in Foreign Lands*, SUN-SENTINEL, Nov. 17, 2000, at 1A.

185 *See, e.g.*, Anti-Atrocity Alien Deportation Act, H.R. 1449, 107th Cong. (2001); Anti-Atrocity Alien Deportation Act, S.864, 107th Cong. (2001).

186 *See generally* M. CHERIF BASSIOUNI, INTERNATIONAL EXTRADITION: UNITED STATES LAW AND PRACTICE (3d ed. 1996).

187 Initial Report of the United States, *supra*, at para. 195.

In the United States, extradition can occur only pursuant to the terms of an extradition agreement.[188] Following a request for extradition, the State Department forwards the request to the Justice Department for execution. The United States Attorney for the federal judicial district where the person is located then seeks an arrest warrant in federal court.[189] Once an individual has been found extraditable by a federal court and after any collateral review of the decision, the extradition request is submitted to the Secretary of State for a final determination.

To date, the United States has not extradited anyone pursuant to the Convention against Torture.[190] The case of *Demjanjuk v. Petrovsky*, however, suggests the potential arguments that may be used by a defendant to challenge such extradition proceedings in the future.[191] In *Demjanjuk*, an alleged Nazi prison camp guard challenged his proposed extradition to Israel on the grounds that Israel lacked jurisdiction to prosecute the murder of Jews in a Nazi extermination camp in Poland during the Second World War.[192] The District Court noted that war crimes and crimes against humanity have long been recognized under international law. Indeed, "[t]he principle that the perpetrators of crimes against humanity and war crimes are subject to universal juris-diction found acceptance in the aftermath of World War II."[193] The Court of Appeals for the Sixth Circuit affirmed the District Court's findings. It concluded that Israel's assertion of universal jurisdiction for war crimes and crimes against humanity was valid under international law. "This universality principle is based on the assumption that some crimes are so universally condemned

---

188 See RESTATEMENT (THIRD), *supra*, at § 478. *But see* Convention against Torture, *supra*, at art. 8(2) ("If a State Party which makes extradition conditional on the existence of a treaty receives a request for extradition from another State Party with which it has no extradition treaty, it may consider this Convention as the legal basis for extradition in respect of such offences. Extradition shall be subject to the other conditions provided by the law of the requested State.").

189 Exigent circumstances, however, may vitiate the need for an arrest warrant.

190 Initial Report of the United States, *supra*, at para. 198.

191 Demjanjuk was alleged to have been the notorious Nazi guard "Ivan the Terrible."

192 Demjanjuk v. Petrovsky, 776 F.2d 571 (6th Cir. 1985).

193 In the Matter of the Extradition of John Demjanjuk, 612 F. Supp. 544, 556 (N.D. Ohio 1985).

that the perpetrators are the enemies of all people. Therefore, any nation which has custody of the perpetrators may punish according to its law applicable to such offenses."[194] Indeed, the Nuremberg legacy makes clear that "there is a jurisdiction over some crimes which extends beyond the territorial limits of any nation."[195] For these reasons, the Court of Appeals affirmed the District Court's decision to deny Demjanjuk's petition for writ of habeas corpus. Demjanjuk was subsequently extradited to Israel.[196]

Surrender proceedings

Similar to extradition, surrender involves the transfer of a suspect to an international tribunal. While the United States has not extradited any foreign national pursuant to the Convention against Torture, it has surrendered one individual to the International Criminal Tribunal for Rwanda ("ICTR").[197] Elizaphan Ntakirutimana was charged by the ICTR with acts of genocide, crimes against humanity, and violations of international humanitarian law that occurred in Rwanda in 1994. Pursuant to the 1995 Agreement on Surrender between the ICTR and the United States ("1995 Agreement"), the ICTR sought Ntakirutimana's

194 *Id.* at 582.

195 *Id.*

196 In 1988, Demjanjuk was tried and convicted in Israel. His conviction was subsequently overturned by the Israeli Supreme Court as a result of new evidence that raised questions about his identity as Ivan the Terrible. As a result, Demjanjuk was returned to the United States. In 1993, the Court of Appeals for the Sixth Circuit strongly criticized the Office of Special Investigations for its handling of the Demjanjuk case. *See* Demjanjuk v. Petrovsky, 10 F.3d 338 (6th Cir. 1993).

In 2001, the OSI initiated new proceedings to denaturalize Demjanjuk, alleging that he did, in fact, participate in acts of persecution as a Nazi concentration camp guard. *See* Eric Fettmann, *The New Demjanjuk Case*, NEW YORK POST, June 6, 2001, at 33.

In 2002, a federal judge revoked Demjanjuk's United States Citizenship, ruling that Demjanjuk knowingly misrepresented his past when he entered the United States in 1952. See David Johnston, *Demjanjuk Loses Citizenship Again: Judge Cites Lies*, NEW YORK TIMES, February 22, 2002, at A16.

197 In April 2001, the Rwandan government submitted an extradition request to the United States for the arrest and transfer of former Rwandan Prime Minister Pierre Rwigema. *See* *Washington Asked to Arrest Ex-Official Linked to Genocide*, CHICAGO TRIB., April 11, 2001, at 6; *Rwanda Orders Arrest of Former Prime Minister for Genocide*, AGENCE FRANCE PRESSE, April 11, 2001.

surrender from the United States.[198] At the time of his indictment, Ntakirutimana was living in the United States, where he had moved to live with relatives. He was subsequently arrested by federal agents in Texas. After a federal magistrate denied the initial request for surrender, the Justice Department supplemented its request for surrender with additional declarations and refiled the request. On this occasion, the Federal District Court certified the surrender to the ICTR. Ntakirutimana's petition for a writ of habeas corpus was denied by the Federal District Court and appealed to the Court of Appeals for the Fifth Circuit. In *Ntakirutimana v. Reno*, the Court of Appeals held that the defendant could be surrendered pursuant to the 1995 Agreement and the subsequent implementing legislation adopted by Congress.[199] According to the Court, the Executive's power to surrender fugitives is not dependent on the existence of an extradition treaty; a congressional-executive agreement is sufficient to establish the power to surrender fugitives. In addition, the Court reiterated the rule that federal courts may only review the sufficiency of evidence in extradition or surrender proceedings for purposes of determining whether probable cause exists. On March 2, 2000, Secretary of State Madeline Albright signed the surrender warrant authorizing Ntakirutimana's transfer to Arusha, Tanzania, for prosecution by the ICTR.[200] Ntakirutimana was formally transferred to the ICTR in March 2000. His trial began in September 2001.

The rule of non-refoulement

If there are any allegations that a fugitive may be tortured if extradited, the Secretary of State is required to make an inquiry

---

198 *See* Agreement on Surrender of Persons Between the Government of the United States and the International Tribunal for the Prosecution of Persons Responsible for Genocide and Other Serious Violations of International Humanitarian Law Committed in the Territory of Rwanda and Rwandan Citizens Responsible for Genocide and Other Such Violations Committed in the Territory of Neighboring States, Jan. 24, 1995, 1996 WL 165484. *See* National Defense Authorization Act, Pub.L. No. 104-106, § 1342, 110 Stat. 486 (1996).

199 Ntakirutimana v. Reno, 184 F.3d 419 (5th Cir. 1999). Although the Court of Appeals refers to *Ntakirutimana* as an extradition case, it is more properly characterized as a surrender case because it involves the transfer of an individual to an international tribunal.

200 U.S. Department of State, Office of the Spokesman, Secretary of State Signs Surrender Warrant (March 24, 2000).

into such allegations.[201] Under the rule of *non-refoulement*, the United States may not extradite an individual to a country where there are substantial grounds for believing he would be in danger of torture.[202] Based on the resulting analysis, the Secretary of State may decide to surrender the fugitive to the requesting state, to deny surrender of the fugitive, or to surrender the fugitive subject to conditions.[203]

The issue of *non-refoulement* in the context of extradition proceedings has been raised on several occasions. The federal courts have indicated that the "rule of non-inquiry" precludes courts from inquiring into the procedures that will be followed in a requesting country or the degree of risk that an extraditee will face after extradition.[204] While several courts have raised the possibility of a humanitarian exception to prevent extradition in cases of possible human rights abuses, it appears that no court has applied this purported exception.[205] In *Cornejo-Barreto v. Seifert*, however, the Court of Appeals for the Ninth Circuit indicated that the decisions of the Secretary of State to extradite an individual who fears torture are reviewable.[206] According to the Court of Appeals, the Foreign Affairs Reform and Restructuring

201 *See* 22 C.F.R. Part 95.

202 On October 21, 1998, Congress adopted the United States Policy with Respect to the Involuntary Return of Persons in Danger of Subjection to Torture as part of the Foreign Affairs Reform and Restructuring Act. *See* Pub. L. No. 105-277, § 2242, 1999 U.S.C.C.A.N. (112 Stat. 2681). According to Section (a), "[i]t shall be the policy of the United States not to expel, extradite, or otherwise effect the involuntary return of any person to a country in which there are substantial grounds for believing the person would be in danger of being subjected to torture, regardless of whether the person is physically present in the United States."

203 According to federal regulations, these determinations by the Secretary of State are not subject to judicial review. 22 C.F.R. § 95.4. *See also* Foreign Affairs Reform and Restructuring Act, Pub.L. No. 105-277, § 2242, 1999 U.S.C.C.A.N. (112 Stat. 2681) 822.

204 *See, e.g.,* Mainero v. Gregg, 164 F.3d 1199 (9th Cir. 1999); Ahmad v. Wigen, 910 F.2d 1063 (2d Cir. 1990). *See generally* John Quigley, *The Rule of Non-Inquiry and Human Rights Treaties*, 45 CATH. U. L. REV. 1213 (1996); Jacques Semmelman, *Federal Courts, the Constitution and the Rule of Non-Inquiry in International Extradition Proceedings*, 76 CORNELL L. REV. 1198 (1991).

205 *See, e.g.,* Lopez-Smith v. Hood, 121 F.3d 1322 (9th Cir. 1997); Emami v. U.S. District Court, 834 F.2d 1444 (9th Cir. 1987); Gallina v. Fraser, 278 F.2d 77 (2d Cir. 1960).

206 Cornejo-Barreto v. Seifert, 218 F.3d 1004 (9th Cir. 2000). *See also* Merisier v. INS, 2000 U.S. Dist. LEXIS 13813 (S.D.N.Y. 2000). *See generally* Zachary Margulis-Ohnuma, *Saying What the Law Is: Judicial Review of Criminal Aliens' Claims Under the Convention against Torture*, 33 N.Y.U. J. INT'L L. & POL. 861 (2001).

Act of 1998 made clear Congress' intention that individuals subject to extradition may not be returned if they are likely to face torture. Despite language in the regulations that purports to preclude judicial review of the extradition decisions by the Secretary of State, the Court of Appeals held that a fugitive fearing torture may petition for review.[207]

Criminal prosecution

When the United States signed the Convention against Torture in 1988, the Reagan administration acknowledged that "the core provisions of the Convention establish a regime for international cooperation in the criminal prosecution of torturers relying on so-called "universal jurisdiction."[208] In its analysis of the Convention against Torture, the State Department reiterated the importance of universal jurisdiction.

> A major concern in drafting Article 5 [of the Convention against Torture], and indeed, in drafting the Convention as a whole, was whether the Convention should provide for possible prosecution by any state in which the alleged offender is found – so-called "universal jurisdiction." The United States strongly supported the provision for universal jurisdiction on the grounds that torture, like hijacking, sabotage, hostage-taking, and attacks on internationally protected persons, is an offense of special international concern, and should have similarly broad, universal recognition as a crime against humanity, with appropriate jurisdictional consequences. Provision for "universal jurisdiction" was also deemed important in view of the fact that the government of the country where official torture actually occurs may seldom be relied upon to take action.[209]

207 Cornejo-Barreto v. Seifert, 218 F.3d at 1014–1016. *But see* Borrero v. INS, 2000 U.S. App. LEXIS 22882 (8th Cir. 2000); Diakite v. INS, 179 F.3d 553 (7th Cir. 1999). For a critique of *Cornejo-Barreto*, see Jacques Semmelman, *International Decisions: Cornejo-Barreto v. Seifert*, 95 AM. J. INT'L L. 435 (2001).

208 Convention against Torture and Other Cruel, Inhuman or Degrading Treatment or Punishment, U.S. Senate, Treaty Doc. 100-20 (1988), at iii [hereinafter "Senate Treaty Document"].

209 *Id.* at 9.

Indeed, the State Department indicated that the "extradite or prosecute" rule set forth in Article 7 was essential to the success of the Convention against Torture. The State Department further emphasized that the notion of universal jurisdiction was not unique; it was patterned after similar provisions in several other international agreements, including the Convention for the Suppression of Unlawful Seizure of Aircraft, the Convention against the Taking of Hostages, and the Convention on the Prevention and Punishment of Crimes against Internationally Protected Persons. The State Department indicated, however, that Article 7 does not require prosecution in every case. "The decision whether to prosecute entails a judgment whether a sufficient legal and factual basis exists for such an action."[210] Moreover, the United States would prefer to extradite individuals to the state where the offense was committed.

Codifying the obligation to extradite or prosecute

In 1994, Congress adopted legislation to criminalize acts of torture, regardless of where such acts occur.[211] Pursuant to 18 U.S.C. § 2340A(a):

> Whoever outside the United States commits or attempts to commit torture shall be fined under this title or imprisoned not more than 20 years, or both, and if death results to any person from conduct prohibited by this subsection, shall be punished by death or imprisoned for any term of years or for life.[212]

210 *Id.* at 11.

211 18 U.S.C. §§ 2340 *et seq.*

212 The definition of "torture" is codified at 18 U.S.C. § 2340 and is consistent with its earlier understanding of the definition of torture set forth in the Convention against Torture:

"'torture' means an act committed by a person acting under the color of law specifically intended to inflict severe physical or mental pain or suffering (other than pain or suffering incidental to lawful sanctions) upon another person within his custody or physical control. . . .

The term 'severe mental pain or suffering' is further defined as the prolonged mental harm caused by or resulting from—

(A) the intentional infliction or threatened infliction of severe physical pain or suffering; (B) the administration or application, or threatened administration or application, of mind altering substances or other procedures calculated to disrupt profoundly the senses or the personality; (C) the threat of imminent death; or (D) the threat that another person will imminently be subjected to death, severe physical pain or suffering or the administration or application of mind altering substances or other procedures calculated to disrupt profoundly the senses or personality; . . . ."

Criminal liability attaches if: (1) the alleged offender is a national of the United States; or (2) the alleged offender is present in the United States, irrespective of the nationality of the victim or alleged offender. In other words, a torturer can be held criminally liable for acts of torture even when such acts occurred abroad and regardless of whether the victim or the perpetrator was a U.S. citizen.

According to the State Department, this legislation was adopted to implement the rule of *aut dedere aut judicare* (extradite or prosecute) as set forth in Article 7 of the Convention against Torture.[213] When an alleged torturer is found in territory under its jurisdiction and the United States does not extradite him or her, the United States acknowledges its obligation to submit the case to its competent authorities for the purpose of prosecution. "Indeed, the U.S. Department of Justice has undertaken measures to ensure that any person on U.S. territory believed to be responsible for acts of torture is identified and handled consistent with the requirements of this provision."[214] In hearings before the Committee against Torture, a U.S. government delegation reaffirmed this commitment to prosecute alleged torturers found in the United States.[215]

U.S. courts have recognized the permissibility of universal jurisdiction in criminal proceedings.[216] In *United States v. Yunis*, for example, the United States alleged that Fawaz Yunis participated in the hijacking and destruction of a foreign-registered aircraft in Lebanon. He was subsequently arrested and transferred to the United States, where he was charged with acts of hostage-taking and hijacking. Yunis challenged his indictment, arguing that the United States lacked jurisdiction to prosecute him for crimes committed abroad. Both the Federal District Court and the Court of Appeals for the District of Columbia denied the petition for habeas corpus relief, affirming U.S. jurisdiction under the Hostage Taking Act and the Hijacking Act.[217] Because there were U.S.

---

213 Initial Report of the United States, *supra*, at paras. 193, 194.

214 *Id.*

215 *See* U.N. Press Release on Committee against Torture, 24th Sess. (May 11, 2000).

216 *See, e.g.,* United States v. Yousef, 927 F. Supp. 673 (S.D.N.Y. 1996). *But see* United States v. Bin Laden, 92 F. Supp. 2d 189 (S.D.N.Y. 2000).

217 *See* 18 U.S.C. § 1203 (hostage taking); 49 U.S.C. § 46502 (hijacking).

nationals on the aircraft, the District Court did not rely exclusively on universal jurisdiction. As noted by the District Court, however, the principle of universal jurisdiction is well-established and provides sufficient basis for asserting jurisdiction over an alleged offender. "In light of the global efforts to punish aircraft piracy and hostage taking, international legal scholars unanimously agree that these crimes fit within the category of heinous crimes for purposes of asserting universal jurisdiction."[218] The Court of Appeals agreed that universal jurisdiction authorizes criminal prosecution, even in the absence of any special connection between the state and the offense. The Court added that "[a]ircraft hijacking may well be one of the few crimes so clearly condemned under the law of nations that states may assert universal jurisdiction to bring offenders to justice, even when the state has no territorial connection to the hijacking and its citizens are not involved."[219]

The problem of ex post facto prosecution

Despite the adoption of legislation criminalizing torture committed outside the United States, no prosecutions have been initiated against alleged torturers pursuant to 18 U.S.C. § 2340A. A key factor in the failure to prosecute is the date on which the alleged crimes were committed. NGOs and the Director of the National Security Unit have noted that many of the cases they have come across involve acts of torture committed prior to 1994. The Justice Department has indicated that it considers prosecuting such cases unconstitutional because they involve acts which at the time they were committed were not criminal under U.S. law.[220]

The *ex post facto* defense, however, is simply inapplicable to actions brought pursuant to 18 U.S.C. § 2340A. The statute does not criminalize what was once innocent conduct. Torture has long been recognized to be a violation of both national and international law, and no country purports to legalize acts of torture. Indeed, a review of domestic legislation throughout the world

---

218 United States v. Yunis, 681 F. Supp. 896, 901 (D.D.C. 1988).

219 United States v. Yunis, 924 F.2d 1086, 1092 (D.C. Cir. 1991).

220 Jody A. Benjamin, *INS Arrests 14 in Rights Abuses in Foreign Lands*, Sun-Sentinel, Nov. 17, 2000, at 1A.

reveals a uniform prohibition against torture and that such pro-
hibitions have existed for many years. Thus, an individual who
committed an act of torture, in any country, cannot possibly argue
that he/she was unaware of the illegal nature of her/his conduct.[221]

The inapplicability of the *ex post facto* defense to acts of
torture is further evidenced by international law. Treaties drafted
to protect human rights, including the International Covenant on
Civil and Political Rights and the European Convention for the
Protection of Human Rights and Fundamental Freedoms, qualify
the *ex post facto* defense in cases involving violations of international law. While international law recognizes the prohibition
against *ex post facto* prosecution, it also recognizes that this
restriction only applies to acts that did not constitute a criminal
offense under national or international law at the time when they
were committed.[222] Indeed, Article 15(2) of the International
Covenant on Civil and Political Rights indicates that "[n]othing in
this article shall prejudice the trial and punishment of any person
for any act or omission which, at the time when it was committed,
was criminal according to the general principles of law recognized
by the community of nations."[223]

The problem of political considerations

Political considerations may also be a factor in the failure of the
U.S. Government to prosecute alleged torturers. In the case of
Tomás Ricardo Anderson Kohatsu, for example, the State Depart-
ment concluded that he could not be prosecuted in the United
States for torture despite overwhelming evidence of his complicity
and the dubious nature of his purported immunity.[224] Anderson

221 *See generally* William J. Aceves, *Prosecuting Human Rights Violations in U.S. Courts: A
Primer for the Justice Department, in* EFFECTIVE STRATEGIES FOR PROTECTING HUMAN RIGHTS (David
Barnhizer ed., 2001). *See also* Peter E. Quint, *The Border Guard Trials and the East German
Past —Seven Arguments*, 48 AM. J. COMP. L. 541 (2000); Eric S. Kobrick, *The Ex Post Facto
Prohibition and the Exercise of Universal Jurisdiction Over International Crimes*, 87 COLUM. L.
REV. 1515 (1987).

222 ICCPR, *supra*, at art. 15(1).

223 *See also* European Convention for the Protection of Human Rights and Fundamental
Freedoms, Nov. 4, 1950, art. 7, 213 U.N.T.S. 221.

224 *See* Aaron Solomon, *The Politics of Prosecutions under the Convention against Torture*, 1
CHI J. INT'L L. 309 (2001).

Kohatsu's status and association with the Organization of American States provided him with no form of diplomatic immunity.[225] Neither the Vienna Convention on Diplomatic Relations nor the Convention on Special Missions extended diplomatic privileges and immunities to Anderson Kohatsu.[226] Similarly, the Agreement Between the Government of the United States of America and the Organization of American States and the Headquarters Agreement Between the Organization of American States and the United States of America did not establish immunity for Anderson Kohatsu.[227] Commenting on the dubious nature of Anderson Kohatsu's purported immunity, one U.S. law enforcement official noted, "[t]his floats up to State and the NSC [National Security Council], and they come back with 'We have to let him walk.'"[228]

Civil litigation

Since 1980, U.S. courts have acknowledged the right of foreign torture victims to seek civil remedies for their injuries. While the United States Government is never a party to these lawsuits, it has occasionally submitted *amicus curiae* (friend of the court) briefs in support of the litigation.

Alien Tort Claims Act

The seminal case is *Filartiga v. Pena-Irala*. In *Filartiga*, two plaintiffs from Paraguay brought a lawsuit in Federal District Court for the Eastern District of New York against a former Paraguayan official for acts of torture committed allegedly against a family member in Paraguay.[229] The lawsuit was brought under the Alien Tort Claims Act, which provides that "[t]he district courts shall

225 *See* Murphy, *Immunity Provided Peruvian Charged with Torture, supra,* at 535.

226 Vienna Convention on Diplomatic Relations, Apr. 18, 1961, 500 U.N.T.S. 95; Convention on Special Missions, Dec. 8, 1969, U.N. Doc. A/7630 (1969).

227 Agreement Between the Government of the United States of America and the Organization of American States, Mar. 20, 1975, TIAS No. 1089, 26 U.S.T. 1025; Headquarters Agreement Between the Organization of American States, S. Treaty Doc. No. 102-40 (May 14, 1992).

228 Karen DeYoung and Lorraine Adams, *US Frees Accused Torturer; Human Rights Groups Decry Ruling on Peruvian,* WASH. POST, March 11, 2000, at A11.

229 Filartiga v. Pena-Irala, 630 F.2d 876 (2d Cir. 1980).

have original jurisdiction of any civil action brought by an alien for a tort only, committed in violation of the law of nations or a treaty of the United States."[230] The District Court dismissed the action on jurisdictional grounds, holding that the term "law of nations," as employed in the Alien Tort Claims Act, excludes the law that governs a state's treatment of its own citizens.

On appeal, the Court of Appeals for the Second Circuit reversed the District Court's ruling and reinstated the lawsuit. After reviewing numerous multilateral, regional, and national sources of law, the Court of Appeals determined that torture was firmly prohibited by international law. "In light of the universal condemnation of torture in numerous international agreements, and the renunciation of torture as an instrument of official policy by virtually all of the nations of the world (in principle if not in practice), we find that an act of torture committed by a state official against one held in detention violates established norms of the international law of human rights, and hence the law of nations."[231] The prohibition against torture protects both nationals and non-nationals. The Court of Appeals also upheld the constitutionality of the Alien Tort Claims Act, recognizing that U.S. courts "regularly adjudicate transitory tort claims between individuals over whom they exercise personal jurisdiction."[232] In addition, Congress had specifically authorized federal court jurisdiction over lawsuits alleging violations of international law by adopting the Alien Tort Claims Act. Since the law of nations formed a part of the common law of the United States, this grant of jurisdiction was authorized by Article III of the Constitution.[233] Accordingly, the Court held that "whenever an alleged torturer is found and served with process by an alien within our borders, §1350 provides federal jurisdiction."[234] Upon remand, the District Court granted the plaintiffs a judgment in excess of $10 million.[235]

230 The Alien Tort Claims Act was enacted as part of the First Judiciary Act of 1789. Judiciary Act of 1789, ch. 20, §9, 1 Stat. 73, 77 (1789) (codified at 28 U.S.C. § 1350).

231 Filartiga, 630 F.2d at 880.

232 Id. at 885.

233 But note Curtis Bradley and Jack L. Goldsmith, Customary International Law as Federal Common Law: A Critique of the Modern Position, 110 HARV. L. REV. 815 (1997).

234 Filartiga, 630 F.2d at 877.

235 Filartiga v. Pena-Irala, 577 F. Supp. 860 (E.D.N.Y. 1984).

Since the *Filartiga* decision, the federal courts have consistently recognized subject matter jurisdiction under the Alien
Tort Claims Act when three conditions are met: (1) an alien sues;
(2) in tort; (3) alleging a violation of international law.[236]

Torture Victim Protection Act

In 1991, Congress adopted the Torture Victim Protection Act
("TVPA") to supplement the remedies available under the Alien
Tort Claims Act and to ensure full compliance with the Convention
against Torture.[237] The TVPA establishes civil liability for acts of
torture and extrajudicial killing committed abroad. The TVPA
provides, in pertinent part that "[a]n individual who, under actual
or apparent authority, or color of law, of any foreign nation—"

> (1) subjects an individual to torture shall, in a civil action,
> be liable for damages to that individual; or
> (2) subjects an individual to extrajudicial killing shall, in a
> civil action, be liable for damages to the individual's legal
> representative, or to any person who may be a claimant
> in an action for wrongful death.

According to the Senate report accompanying the TVPA, torture
violates standards of conduct accepted by virtually every nation
and this prohibition has attained the status of customary international law. "These universal principles provide little comfort,
however, to the thousands of victims of torture and summary
executions around the world. . . . Despite universal condemnation
of these abuses, many of the world's governments still engage in or
tolerate torture of their citizens. . . ."[238] The TVPA was adopted to
address these problems.

236 *See, e.g.,* Doe v. Unocal, 963 F. Supp. 880 (C.D. Cal. 1997); Abebe-Jira v. Negewo, 72 F.3d
844 (11th Cir. 1996); Kadic v. Karadzic, 70 F.3d 232 (2d Cir. 1995); Hilao v. Marcos, 25 F.3d 1467
(9th Cir. 1995); Trajano v. Marcos, 978 F.2d 493 (9th Cir. 1992); Siderman de Blake v. Republic
of Argentina, 965 F.2d 699 (9th Cir. 1992). *But see* Tel-Oren v. Libyan Arab Republic, 726 F.2d
774 (D.C. Cir. 1984), *cert. denied,* 470 U.S. 1003 (1985).

237 Pub. L. No. 102-256, 106 Stat. 73, *reprinted in* 28 U.S.C. § 1350 notes.

238 S. Rep. No. 249, 102d Cong., 1st Sess. (1991). *See also* H.R. Rep. No. 367, 102d Cong., 1st.
Sess., pt. 1 (1991). On signing the TVPA into law, President Bush acknowledged the importance
of providing a civil remedy to victims of torture. "In this new era, in which countries
throughout the world are turning to democratic institutions and the rule of law, we must
maintain and strengthen our commitment to ensuring that human rights are respected
everywhere." Statement on Signing the Torture Victim Protection Act of 1991, Mar. 12, 1992, 28
WEEKLY COMP. PRES. DOC. 465, 466 (Mar. 16, 1992).

The TVPA differs from the Alien Tort Claims Act in several respects. Unlike the earlier statute, the TVPA is not limited to plaintiffs who are foreign nationals but allows U.S. citizens to pursue civil actions as well. However, the TVPA only allows civil actions for torture or extrajudicial killing perpetrated by officials of foreign governments; the Alien Tort Claims Act contains no such restriction.

Well over 70 lawsuits have been filed pursuant to the Alien Tort Claims Act and the Torture Victim Protection Act seeking civil remedies for violations of international human rights norms, including the prohibition against torture. These lawsuits have been filed against a variety of defendants, including foreign government officials, multinational corporations, and private individuals. Several of these lawsuits have resulted in significant damage awards, although most plaintiffs have been unable to recover the amounts awarded, either because the defendants are without funds or they reside abroad.[239]

The Foreign Sovereign Immunities Act

While the Alien Tort Claims Act and the Torture Victim Protection Act authorize civil actions against public officials and private individuals, they do not provide jurisdiction for actions against foreign governments. The Foreign Sovereign Immunities Act ("FSIA") is the sole basis for obtaining jurisdiction over a foreign state in U.S. courts.[240] Under the FSIA, a foreign state is presumed to be immune from suit unless one or more of the codified exceptions to immunity exist.[241] In 1996, Congress amended the FSIA to provide authorization for lawsuits against foreign states that allege, *inter alia*, acts of torture, extrajudicial killing, hostage taking, or aircraft sabotage.[242] However, three conditions must be

---

239 *See* BETH STEPHENS & MICHAEL RATNER, INTERNATIONAL HUMAN RIGHTS LITIGATION IN U.S. COURTS 239 (1996); Richard B. Lillich, *Damages for Gross Violations of International Human Rights Awarded by U.S. Courts*, 15 HUM. RTS Q. 207 (1993).

240 Amerada Hess Shipping Corp. v. Argentine Republic 488 U.S. 428 (1989).

241 28 U.S.C. § 1604. Pursuant to 28 U.S.C. § 1605, these exceptions include situations of waiver, commercial activity, limited property rights, and arbitration.

242 28 U.S.C. § 1607.

met in order to bring these actions: (1) the plaintiff or victim must be a United States national; (2) the foreign state must have been designated as a state sponsor of terrorism by the State Department; and (3) the foreign state must be offered an opportunity to arbitrate the claims if the actionable conduct occurred within that state's territory. Litigants who cannot fulfill these three conditions cannot pursue civil actions against foreign governments who commit or authorize acts of torture. Several lawsuits have been brought under the state-sponsored terrorism exception to the FSIA, which have resulted in significant damage awards.[243] Congress recently adopted legislation that authorizes the payment of certain FSIA judgments from the U.S. Treasury.[244] Several of these payments have been made.[245]

The challenges to civil litigation

Various challenges have been made against civil lawsuits alleging human rights violations, including the political question doctrine, the act of state doctrine, and the doctrine of *forum non conveniens.*[246] The political question doctrine provides that courts

---

243 These cases involved acts of terrorism, including hostage-taking and extrajudicial killing. *See* Jenco v. Islamic Republic of Iran, 2001 U.S. Dist. LEXIS 11025 (D.D.C. 2001); Sutherland v. Islamic Republic of Iran, 2001 U.S. Dist. LEXIS 8539 (D.D.C. 2001); Elahi v. Islamic Republic of Iran, 124 F. Supp. 2d 97 (D.D.C. 2000); Daliberti v. Republic of Iraq, 97 F. Supp. 2d 38 (D.D.C. 2000); Anderson v. Islamic Republic of Iran, 90 F. Supp. 2d 107 (D.D.C. 2000); Cicippio v. Islamic Republic of Iran, 18 F. Supp. 2d 62 (D.D.C. 1998); Flatow v. Islamic Republic of Iran, 999 F. Supp. 1 (D.D.C. 1998); Alejandre v. Republic of Cuba, 996 F. Supp. 1239 (S.D. Fla. 1997); Rein v. Socialist People's Libyan Arab Jamahiriya, 162 F.3d 748 (2d Cir. 1999).

244 *See* Victims of Trafficking and Violence Protection Act of 2000, 106 Pub. L. No. 386, § 2002, 114 Stat. 1464. *See generally* Sean P. Vitrano, *Hell-Bent on Awarding Recovery to Terrorism Victims: The Evolution and Application of the Antiterrorism Amendments to the Foreign Sovereign Immunities Act,* 19 DICKINSON J. INT'L L. 213 (2001).

245 *U.S. Approves Payment of Frozen Cuban Assets to Relatives of Brothers to Rescue,* 17 INT'L ENFORCEMENT L. REP. (2001); Jay Weaver, *U.S. Okays Release of Cuban Assets to Pay Families of Shot-Down Pilots,* MIAMI HERALD, Feb. 14, 2001; Bruce Zagaris, *U.S. Starts Implementation of Payment to Terrorist Victims and Iran Approves Lawsuits against U.S.,* 16 INT'L ENFORCEMENT L. REP. 1057 (Dec. 2000).

246 *See generally* Kathryn Lee Boyd, *The Inconvenience of Victims: Abolishing Forum Non Conveniens in U.S. Human Rights Litigation,* 39 VA. J. INT'L L. 41 (1998); Russell Weintraub, *Establishing Incredible Events by Credible Evidence: Civil Suits for Atrocities That Violate International Law,* 62 BROOK. L. REV. 753 (1996); Ralph Steinhardt, *Human Rights Litigation and the "One Voice" Orthodoxy in Foreign Affairs, in* WORLD JUSTICE? U.S. COURTS AND INTERNATIONAL HUMAN RIGHTS 23 (Mark Gibney ed., 1991).

should not consider cases that may infringe upon the authority of the executive or legislative branches of government. The act of state doctrine posits that U.S. courts should not review the validity of the actions of foreign governments taken in their territory. Under the doctrine of *forum non conveniens*, U.S. courts should dismiss lawsuits where an adequate alternate forum exists and where a balance of public and private interest factors indicates that domestic adjudication is inappropriate. With few exceptions, the courts have generally dismissed these challenges.[247]

Immigration restrictions

Under international law, individuals who have committed egregious human rights violations are not eligible for certain forms of immigration relief.[248] For example, the 1951 Convention Relating to the Status of Refugees ("Refugee Convention") precludes refugee status to any person with respect to whom there are serious reasons for considering that:

> (a) He has committed a crime against peace, a war crime, or a crime against humanity, as defined in the international instruments drawn up to make provision in respect of such crimes;
> (b) He has committed a serious non-political crime outside the country of refuge prior to his admission to that country as a refugee;
> (c) He has been guilty of acts contrary to the purposes and principles of the United Nations.[249]

These provisions preclude refugee protection for individuals who, by their conduct, are not deserving of refugee status.

---

247 *See, e.g.*, Doe v. Unocal, 963 F. Supp. 880 (C.D. Cal. 1997); Abebe-Jira v. Negewo, 72 F.3d 844 (11th Cir. 1996); Kadic v. Karadzic, 70 F.3d 232 (2d Cir. 1995).

248 *See generally* GUY GOODWIN-GILL, THE REFUGEE IN INTERNATIONAL LAW 95 (2d ed. 1996); Symposium, *Special Supplementary Issue on Exclusion*, 12 INT'L J. REFUGEE L. 1 (2000).

249 Convention Relating to the Status of Refugees, July 28, 1951, art. 1(F), 189 U.N.T.S. 150. *See also* GOODWIN-GILL, *supra*, at 95. Even crimes committed out of a genuine political motive will not be considered non-political crimes if they are disproportionate to the objective or are of an atrocious or barbarous nature. *Id.* at 101–108. *See generally* Michael Kingsley Nyinah, *Exclusion Under Article 1F: Some Reflections on Context, Principles, and Practice*, 12 INT'L J. REFUGEE L. 295 (2000).

According to the United Nations High Commissioner for Refugees, "[a]t the time when the Convention was drafted, the memory of the trials of major war criminals was still very much alive, and there was agreement on the part of States that war criminals should not be protected."[250] In addition to the Refugee Convention, the 1969 Convention Governing the Specific Aspects of Refugee Problems in Africa adopted by the Organization of African Unity contains a similar exclusion provision.[251] Significantly, these exclusion provisions apply regardless of the other merits of a refugee's claim.[252]

The United Nations High Commissioner for Refugees ("UNHCR") has acknowledged the importance of using exclusion provisions to protect the legitimacy of the refugee process. The Statute of the Office of the United Nations High Commissioner for Refugees provides that the competence of the High Commissioner shall not extend to a person "[i]n respect of whom there are serious reasons for considering that he has committed a crime covered by the provisions of treaties of extradition or a crime mentioned in article VI of the London Charter of the International Military Tribunal or by the provisions of article 14, paragraph 2, of the Universal Declaration of Human Rights."[253] The UNHCR Handbook on Procedures and Criteria for Determining Refugee Status makes a similar determination.[254] Given the complex nature of exclusion cases, however, the UNHCR has emphasized that the exclusion provisions must be narrowly interpreted.[255] Moreover, "exclusion clauses should not be used to determine the admissibility of an application or claim for refugee status. Any preliminary or automatic exclusion would have the effect of denying such individual an assessment of the claim for refugee

---

250 UNITED NATIONS HIGH COMMISSIONER FOR REFUGEES, HANDBOOK ON PROCEDURES AND CRITERIA FOR DETERMINING REFUGEE STATUS para. 148 (1996) [hereinafter "UNHCR HANDBOOK"].

251 Convention Governing the Specific Aspects of Refugee Problems in Africa, Sept. 10, 1969, 1001 U.N.T.S. 45.

252 GOODWIN-GILL, *supra*, at 97. *See also Symposium Issue: Exclusion from Protection*, 12 INT'L J. REFUGEE L. 1 (2000); Nancy Weisman, *Article 1(F) of the 1951 Convention Relating to the Status of Refugees in Canadian Law*, 8 INT'L J. REFUGEE L. 111 (1996).

253 Statute of the Office of the United Nations High Commissioner for Refugees, Dec. 14, 1950, art. 7(d), U.N. Doc. A/1775 (1950).

254 UNHCR HANDBOOK, *supra*, at paras. 140–163.

255 *Id.* para. 149.

status."[256] Accordingly, the UNHCR has called for the inclusion before exclusion principle in cases of refugee determination—"the applicability of the exclusion clauses should be considered only once it is determined (individually or *prima facie*) that the criteria for refugee status are satisfied."[257]

The Inter-American Commission on Human Rights has also recognized restrictions on the right of asylum.[258] The Inter-American Commission has indicated that "the institution of asylum is totally subverted by granting such protection to persons who leave their country to elude a determination of their liability as the material or intellectual author of international crimes."[259] Accordingly, the Inter-American Commission recommends that OAS states "refrain from granting asylum to any person alleged to be the material or intellectual author of international crimes."[260]

The Immigration and Nationality Act

The Immigration and Nationality Act ("INA") contains several provisions that limit the scope of immigration relief available to individuals who commit serious violations of international human rights norms. For example, a person who "ordered, incited, assisted, or otherwise participated in the persecution of any person" on account of race, religion, nationality, political opinion, or membership in a particular social group, may not be classified as a refugee and is barred from a grant of asylum.[261] This provision is consistent with the exclusion clause of the Refugee Convention and has been applied to deny asylum status in several cases.[262]

In 1978, Congress adopted the Holtzman Amendment to preclude all forms of immigration relief to individuals who

256 *See* Memorandum from the United Nations High Commissioner for Refugees on the Applicability of Exclusion Clauses 3 (Dec. 2, 1996).

257 *Id.*

258 INTER-AMERICAN COMMISSION ON HUMAN RIGHTS, ASYLUM AND INTERNATIONAL CRIMES (2000).

259 *Id.*

260 *Id.*

261 8 U.S.C. § 1101(a)(42); 8 U.S.C. § 1158(b)(2).

262 *See, e.g.,* Riad v. INS, 1998 U.S. App. LEXIS 21452 (9th Cir. 1998); Han v. INS, 1997 U.S. App. LEXIS 3854 (9th Cir. 1997); Ofosu v. McElroy, 98 F.3d 694 (2d Cir. 1996); McMullen v. INS, 788 F.2d 591 (9th Cir. 1986).

participated in acts of Nazi persecution.[263] The legislation was adopted in response to a growing awareness that former Nazi persecutors had entered the United States after World War II and, on several occasions, had become naturalized U.S. citizens.[264] The Holtzman Amendment precludes admission and facilitates deportation of individuals who participated in Nazi persecution.[265] It also prevents the Attorney General from authorizing cancellation of removal or granting voluntary departure to aliens who have committed these acts. In addition, the Office of Special Investigations ("OSI") was established to investigate and prosecute any individual who had assisted or participated in Nazi persecution.[266] To date, the OSI has investigated over 1,600 people and

---

263 *See generally* Bruce Einhorn et al., *The Prosecution of War Criminals and Violators of Human Rights in the United States*, 19 WHITTIER L. REV. 281 (1997); Matthew Lippman, *Fifty Years After Auschwitz: Prosecutions of Nazi Death Camp Defendants*, 11 CONN. J. INT'L L. 199 (1996); Marc J. Hertzberg, *Prosecuting Nazi War Criminals: A Call for the Immediate Prosecution of Living Nazi War Criminals*, 5 MD. J. CONTEMP. LEGAL ISSUES 181 (1993/1994); Jeffrey N. Mausner, *Apprehending and Prosecuting Nazi War Criminals in the United States*, 15 NOVA L. REV. 747 (1991); Elliott M. Abramson, *Reflections on the Unthinkable: Standards Relating to the Denaturalization and Deportation of Nazis and Those Who Collaborated with the Nazis During World War II*, 57 U. CIN. L. REV. 1311 (1989); Robert A. Cohen, *United States Exclusion and Deportation of Nazi War Criminals: The Act of October 30, 1978*, 13 N.Y.U. J. INT'L L. & POL. 101 (1980).

264 *See generally*, ALAN ROSENBAUM, PROSECUTING NAZI WAR CRIMINALS (1993); ALLAN RYAN, QUIET NEIGHBORS: PROSECUTING NAZI WAR CRIMINALS IN AMERICA (1984); Stephen Massey, *Individual Responsibility for Assisting the Nazis in Persecuting Civilians*, 71 MINN. L. REV. 97 (1986).

265 8 U.S.C. § 1182(a)(3)(E)(i); 8 U.S.C. § 1227(a)(4)(D).

266 *See* Transfer of Functions of the Special Litigation Unit Within the Immigration and Naturalization Service of the Department of Justice to the Criminal Division of the Department of Justice, Order of the U.S. Attorney General, No. 851-79 (Sept. 4, 1979) [hereinafter "Transfer of Functions Order"].
   Pursuant to the terms of the 1979 Attorney General Order, OSI was granted "the primary responsibility for detecting, investigating, and, where appropriate, taking legal action to deport, denaturalize, or prosecute any individual who was admitted as an alien into or became a naturalized citizen of the United States and who had assisted the Nazis by persecuting any person because of race, religion, national origin, or political opinion." Specifically, the OSI shall:
   1. Review pending and new allegations that individuals, who prior to and during World War II, under the supervision or in association with the Nazi government in Germany, its allies, and other affiliated governments, ordered, incited, assisted, or otherwise participated in the persecution of any person because of race, religion, national origin or political opinion;
   2. Investigate, as appropriate, each allegation to determine whether there is sufficient evidence to file a complaint to revoke citizenship, support a show cause order to deport, or seek an indictment or any other judicial process against any such individuals;
   3. Maintain liaison with foreign prosecution, investigation and intelligence offices;

filed approximately 100 cases seeking denaturalization or deportation of former Nazis.[267] It has also used the Holtzman Amendment to deny entry to former Nazis and individuals who participated in acts of Nazi persecution.[268] Recently, the OSI has used the Nazi persecution statutes to prevent Japanese war criminals from entering the United States.[269]

    In 1990, Congress extended the Holtzman Amendment provisions to individuals who participated in genocide.[270] While the legislative history is silent, it appears that this provision was added in response to U.S. ratification of the Convention on the Prevention and Punishment of the Crime of Genocide in 1988.[271] The International Religious Freedom Act of 1998 established similar immigration restrictions for any individual who, while serving as a foreign government official, was responsible for particularly severe violations of religious freedom.[272] This provision only applies, however, to foreign government officials who have committed such acts in the preceding 24-month period.

4. Use appropriate Government agency resources and personnel for investigations, guidance, information and analysis; and

5. Direct and coordinate the investigation, prosecution, and any other legal actions instituted in these cases with the Immigration and Naturalization Service, the Federal Bureau of Investigation, the United States Attorneys Offices, and other relevant Federal agencies.

Transfer of Functions Order, *supra*, at 3.

267 *See, e.g.*, United States v. Balsys, 524 U.S. 666 (1998); United States v. Gecas, 120 F.3d 1419 (11th Cir. 1997); Kungys v. United States 485 U.S. 759 (1988); Schellong v. I.N.S., 805 F.2d 655 (7th Cir. 1986).

268 *See, e.g.*, Philip Shenon, *U.S. Disputes Waldheim Assertions*, NEW YORK TIMES, Feb. 17, 1998, at A3; *U.S. Bars Kurt Waldheim, Cites Service with Nazis*, CHICAGO TRIBUNE, Apr. 28, 1987, at C1. *See also* Michael Janofsky, *Chilean Equestrian Sued in U.S. Court*, NEW YORK TIMES, Aug. 15, 1987, at A48; Michael Janofsky, *Visa Denial: A Basic Conflict*, NEW YORK TIMES, Aug. 14, 1987, at B14.

269 *See* James Dao, *U.S. Bars Japanese Who Admits War Crime*, NEW YORK TIMES, June 27, 1998, at A3; Ronald J. Ostrow, *U.S. Bars 2 Repentant Japan Veterans*, LOS ANGELES TIMES, June 25, 1998, at A9.

270 *See* 8 U.S.C. § 1182(a)(3)(E)(ii). *See generally* Paul John Chrisopoulos, *Giving Meaning to the Term "Genocide" as It Applies to U.S. Immigration Policy*, 17 LOY. L.A. INT'L & COMP. L.J. 925 (1995).

271 Convention on the Prevention and Punishment of the Crime of Genocide, Dec. 9, 1948, 78 U.N.T.S. 277.

272 *See* International Religious Freedom Act, Pub. L. No. 105-292, 112 Stat. 2787 (1998); 8 U.S.C. § 1182(a)(2)(G). *See generally* T. Jeremy Gunn, *A Preliminary Response to Criticisms of the International Religious Freedom Act of 1998*, 2000 B.Y.U. L. REV. 841 (2000).

The limits of the Immigration and Nationality Act

In contrast, perpetrators of other human rights violations such as torture or extrajudicial killing are not subject to the same set of immigration restrictions that apply to former Nazis. These individuals can be excluded or deported only if they fall within the general class of excludable or deportable aliens, which includes the following categories: crimes involving moral turpitude; terrorist activities; foreign policy implications; membership in a totalitarian party; or misrepresentation.[273] According to the Justice Department, however, these provisions do not provide the INS with sufficient authority to respond to human rights abusers. "[T]he present state of immigration law often does not provide the INS with the necessary tools to remove individuals from the United States, even when they have allegedly committed acts considered to be atrocious human rights abuses."[274] These limitations even apply to acts of genocide or violations of religious freedom.

> For example, genocide applies only to actions committed against a national, ethnic, racial or religious group. To constitute genocide, those actions also have to be committed with the specific intent of destroying a protected group in whole or in part. Further, the genocide bar applies only to those "engaged" in genocide, which arguably does not include those who may have incited, assisted, conspired or attempted to engage in genocide. Similarly, to be barred for particularly severe violations of religious freedom, the individual must be a foreign official who has engaged in those violations in the last twenty-four months. Those who have "ordered, incited, assisted or otherwise participated in" persecution are statutorily barred from admission as a refugee and from obtaining asylum status or withholding of removal, but they are eligible to enter the United States, to adjust their status to lawful permanent residence, and to obtain United States citizenship.[275]

273 See INA Section 212(a)(2)(A) (acts of moral turpitude); INA Section 212(a)(3)(B) (terrorist activity); INA Section 212(a)(3)(C) (foreign policy consequences); INA Section 212(a)(2)(D) (membership in totalitarian party); INA Section 212(a)(6)(C) (misrepresentation).

274 Castello Testimony, supra, at 21, 22. See also David Adams, Reaching for More Foreign Criminals, ST. PETERSBURG TIMES, Apr. 9, 2001, at 1A.

275 Castello Testimony, supra, at 22.

The National Security Unit of the Immigration and Naturalization Service

The Immigration and Naturalization Service has indicated that the investigation, prosecution, and removal of aliens who are human rights abusers is one of its highest enforcement priorities. Yet the National Security Unit, which is the component within the INS responsible for coordinating investigations into suspected human rights abusers, may lack the resources and mechanisms to effectively carry out this task. For example, the NSU is responsible for two other rather substantial areas of jurisdiction: international terrorism and foreign counterintelligence.[276] There are no appropriations for coordinating investigations into suspected human rights abusers—funding is leveraged from the counter-terrorism budget. [277] Furthermore, there is no established procedure for torture victims to follow if they want to provide information about suspected torturers to the National Security Unit or any other federal government agency.

The rule of non-refoulement

In cases where an individual may be tortured if removed from the United States, the Justice Department has adopted regulations to comply with the rule of *non-refoulement* as set forth in the Convention against Torture.[278] These regulations permit individuals to raise a claim of *non-refoulement* during the course of removal proceedings.[279] Most cases involving *non-refoulement* are initially determined by Immigration Judges of the Executive

---

276 Letter from Walter D. Cadman, Director, National Security Unit, Immigration and Naturalization Service to William F. Schulz, Executive Director, Amnesty International USA (September 6, 2001).

277 Presentation of Walter D. Cadman, Director, National Security Unit, Immigration and Naturalization Service at Forensic Training Institute: Torture Survivors and the Legal Process (Nov. 16, 2001).

278 These regulations were adopted pursuant to the Foreign Affairs Reform and Restructuring Act of 1998. *See* 8 C.F.R. Parts 3, 103, 208, 235, 238, 240, 241, and 253. These provisions are distinct from the protections against *non-refoulement* established by Congress pursuant to the Convention Relating to the Status of Refugees. *See* 8 U.S.C. § 1158. *See also* DEBORAH ANKER, LAW OF ASYLUM IN THE UNITED STATES 465 (3d ed. 1999).

279 *See generally* Al-Saher v. INS, 268 F.3d 1143 (9th Cir. 2001); Kamalthas v. INS, 251 F.3d 1279 (9th Cir. 2001); Khourassany v. INS, 208 F.3d 1096 (9th Cir. 2000).

Office for Immigration Review and are subject to review by the Board of Immigration Appeals. The burden of proof is on the applicant "to establish that it is more likely than not that he . . . would be tortured if removed to the proposed country of removal."[280] In assessing whether an applicant would be tortured in the proposed country of removal, the regulations list the following criteria for consideration: (1) evidence of past torture inflicted upon the applicant; (2) evidence that the applicant could relocate to a part of the country of removal where he or she is not likely to be tortured; (3) evidence of gross, flagrant or mass violations of human rights within the country of removal, where applicable; and (4) other relevant information regarding conditions in the country of removal.[281] If an individual meets these criteria, she/he is entitled to withholding of removal. If an individual is ineligible for withholding of removal because of certain activity, such as her/his participation in acts of genocide or Nazi persecution, the regulations authorize deferral of removal, a more temporary form of protection.[282] Deferral of removal differs from withholding of deportation in several respects. Perhaps most significantly, the termination process for deferral of removal is quicker than for withholding of deportation. In addition, the regulations provide for the possibility that the Secretary of State may forward to the Attorney General assurances obtained from the government of a specific country that an individual would not be tortured if removed to that country.[283]

280 8 C.F.R. § 208.16(c)(2).
281 8 C.F.R. § 208.16(c)(3).
282 8 C.F.R. § 208.17.
283 8 C.F.R. § 208.18(c).

7: Protecting victims of torture

"I am afraid that the moment I go outside, interrogation and torture will come back. I cannot come back to my intellectual life. I cannot read poetry anymore, because reading poetry is an experience full of feelings."
—Jacobo Timerman[284]
Torture survivor from Argentina

Every day, survivors of human rights abuses arrive in the United States from throughout the world. These individuals reflect the patterns of oppression worldwide—Bosnia, East Timor, El Salvador, Guatemala, Rwanda, Sierra Leone, Somalia. On average, 20% of all refugees fleeing countries that use torture are themselves victims of torture. By some estimates, over 400,000 victims of torture now reside in the United States.[285] As noted by the Office of Refugee Resettlement, "[t]he psychosocial and health consequences of violence and traumatic stress have emerged as one of the public health problems of our time."[286]

The trauma of torture

Survivors of torture have lived through experiences filled with excruciating pain, constant fear of death, gross humiliation, and other assaults on their humanity.[287] Severe beatings appear to be the most common form of torture. These are often combined with other violent acts, including severe shaking, whipping, burning, electrocution, and sexual assault. Other forms of torture may leave no physical marks, but the suffering they cause is no less severe. These methods include starvation, sleep deprivation, mock

---

284 Joseph P. Fried, *Brooklyn Court Told of Torture of Paraguayan*, New York Times, Feb. 13, 1982, at 27.

285 Initial Report of the United States, *supra*, at para. 285.

286 Discretionary Funds for Assistance for Treatment of Torture Survivors, 66 Fed. Reg. 13771 (March 7, 2001).

287 *See generally* Center for Victims of Torture, Survivors of Politically Motivated Torture: A Large Growing, and Invisible Population of Crime Victims (2000); Metin Basoglu, *Prevention of Torture and Care of Survivors*, 270 J. Am. Med. Ass'n. 606 (1993).

executions, asphyxiation, drowning, sensory deprivation, and the use of drugs. Even threats to family members or individuals close to the victim cause significant suffering. Throughout these acts, torturers demand that their victims make impossible choices that result in the breakdown of their moral codes. Those who manage to escape these horrific acts carry with them the acute and long-term effects of torture.

Systematic medical studies reveal significant physiological trauma suffered by victims of torture.[288] Physicians regularly document paralysis, fractured bones, severed limbs, burned skin, organ damage, and countless other physical ailments caused by torture. Musculoskeletal injuries are common. Victims of cranial trauma suffer from impaired vision, loss of hearing, and neurological damage. Victims of sexual assault often suffer sterility and impotence. Few victims of torture escape without a permanent, physical reminder of their ordeal. Others share a different fate, however, when torture becomes murder.

Medical studies have also chronicled the severe psychological effects of torture.[289] Victims of torture often suffer anxiety, depression, and guilt.[290] Suicidal thoughts are common. Many survivors experience post-traumatic stress disorder, where they persistently reexperience the trauma of torture in flashbacks and nightmares. The past can break into the present at any time—a painful and disorienting phenomenon triggered by the sight of someone wearing a uniform, a small enclosed area, or numerous other reminders of torture. To avoid nightmares, many survivors avoid sleeping. For a survivor repeatedly pushed into a vat of water and nearly drowned, the sight of rain can be unbearable. For others, uncertainties involved in waiting for an appointment to begin can be traumatic. A survivor of electric shock torture may not be able to tolerate the sight of electrical equipment. Common activities, such as reading a

---

288 See METIN BASOGLU, TORTURE AND ITS CONSEQUENCES: CURRENT TREATMENT APPROACHES (1992); THE BREAKING OF BODIES AND MINDS: TORTURE, PSYCHIATRIC ABUSE, AND THE HEALTH PROFESSIONS (Eric Stover & Elena Nightingale, eds. 1985).

289 G. VAN DER VEER, COUNSELING AND THERAPY WITH REFUGEES AND VICTIMS OF TRAUMA: PSYCHOLOGICAL PROBLEMS OF VICTIMS OF WAR, TORTURE, AND REPRESSION (2d ed. 1998).

290 See generally Angela Burnett & Michael Peel, The Health of Survivors of Torture and Organised Violence, 322 BR. MED. J. 606 (March 10, 2001).

newspaper or watching television, may appear threatening as potential reminders of the violence suffered. In attempting to avoid painful memories or extreme stress, survivors may isolate themselves from familiar people and situations. An emotional numbing can occur. At the same time, survivors often carry out daily activities in an "emergency mode," constantly on their guard. Hyperalertness and exaggerated responses to startling sounds or sights continue to plague many survivors. A general lack of trust and a sense of extreme vulnerability may characterize a survivor's experience of the surrounding world in the aftermath of torture. These psychological symptoms, often requiring treatment long after physical wounds have healed, can seriously impair a survivor's ability to resume social relationships, occupational roles, and other aspects of everyday life. Alcoholism and drug abuse often complicate this clinical picture as survivors try to numb their pain.

The shattering trauma of torture remains, in widely varying forms and to many different degrees, with all survivors. No measure of compensation can restore fully what the torturer took from them. But experiences of understanding, support, and justice can accelerate their recovery from torture. Recovery of the self-esteem, self-confidence, and aspirations torn from them during torture, however, requires long-term treatment.

Treatment and rehabilitation

The importance of providing treatment and rehabilitation to torture victims has gradually been acknowledged by the international community. In 1981, the United Nations established the Voluntary Fund for Victims of Torture to receive contributions from states and individuals for distribution to humanitarian, legal, and financial programs that assist victims of torture.[291] To be selected, a project must provide medical, psychological, social, financial, or legal assistance to torture victims and their families. A project may also be selected if it provides training to health professionals or facilitates the organization of conferences devoted to torture victims. At its May 2001 session, the Board of

291 General Assembly Resolution 36/151 (1981).

Trustees that administers the Fund distributed $8 million in grants to 200 organizations.[292]

In 1982, Amnesty International established the first torture treatment center, the Rehabilitation and Research Centre for Torture Victims, in Copenhagen, Denmark. Since it was established, the Center has provided treatment to thousands of torture victims. Today, approximately 200 rehabilitation centers and related programs for torture victims exist throughout the world. Many of these programs receive assistance from the United Nations Voluntary Fund for Victims of Torture.

In the United States, there are approximately 20 centers for the treatment of torture victims. The Center for Victims of Torture in Minneapolis was established in 1985 and was one of the first U.S. centers to focus exclusively on the care and support of torture victims. The Center treats 150 clients annually, providing medical care, physical therapy, psychiatric care, psychotherapy, social services, and legal assistance. It also conducts research programs and extensive training programs for professionals serving survivors in both the United States and abroad. Other prominent torture treatment centers in the United States include the Marjorie Kovler Center for the Treatment of Survivors of Torture in Chicago, Survivors International in San Francisco, and the Bellevue/NYU Program for Survivors of Torture in New York City.

Recognizing the importance of treatment and rehabilitation programs for victims of torture, Congress adopted the Torture Victims Relief Act in October 1998.[293] In its findings, Congress noted that a significant number of refugees and asylum-seekers entering the United States have been victims of torture. These individuals "should be provided with the rehabilitation services which would enable them to become productive members of our communities."[294] Indeed, "[b]y acting to help the survivors of torture and protect their families, the United States can help to

---

292 Press Release, United Nations, High Commissioner for Human Rights Approves $8 million in Grants for Torture Survivors (June 22, 2001).

293 Torture Victims Relief Act of 1998, Pub. L. No. 105-320, 112 Stat. 3017.

294 *See* 22 U.S.C. § 2152 (History; Ancillary Laws and Directives).

heal the effects of torture and prevent its use around the world."[295] The Act authorized the distribution of $31 million over a two-year period for investment in domestic and foreign torture treatment centers and for contributions to the United Nations Voluntary Fund for Victims of Torture. Specifically, the Torture Victims Relief Act allocated $12.5 million for torture treatment centers abroad and $12.5 million for centers in the United States. In addition, $6 million was allocated for the United Nations Voluntary Fund for Victims of Torture. Other provisions of the Act included special immigration considerations for survivors of torture and training for foreign service and immigration officers to build their skills in interviewing survivors and gathering evidence of torture. Finally, the Act urged the President, acting through the U.S. Representative to the United Nations, to support the work of the Committee against Torture and the Special Rapporteur on Torture.

In October 1999, Congress adopted the Torture Victims Relief Reauthorization Act.[296] The Act authorizes $45 million over a three-year period for investment in domestic treatment centers for victims of torture and for contributions to the United Nations Voluntary Fund for Victims of Torture. Specifically, the Act authorized the appropriation of $30 million for domestic treatment centers and $15 million for the United Nations Voluntary Fund for Victims of Torture.[297]

In its May 2000 Concluding Observations on the Initial Report of the United States, the Committee against Torture acknowledged the efforts of the United States to assist torture victims, citing with approval the "broad legal recourse to compensation for victims of torture, whether or not such torture occurred in the United States of America" as well as its generous contributions to the U.N. Voluntary Fund.[298]

---

295 Id.

296 Torture Victims Relief Reauthorization Act of 1999, Pub. L. No. 06-87, § 1, 113 Stat. 1301.

297 In 2000, the House Appropriations Committee recommended the specific disbursement of $10 million for the Agency for International Development to support foreign treatment centers for victims of torture. See House Report 106-720, Foreign Operations, Export Financing, and Related Programs, Appropriations Bill, 2001, 106th Cong., 2d Session (2000).

298 Committee against Torture, Conclusions and Observations of the Committee against Torture: United States of America, U.N. Doc. CAT/C/24/6.

8: A comparative perspective

"I survived those years in the camps. This is for those who didn't survive."
—**Kemal Mehinovic**[299]

Torture survivor from Bosnia-Herzegovina

Many countries are grappling with the challenge of developing and implementing effective strategies to combat impunity. It is instructive, therefore, to examine how other countries have addressed this problem.[300]

The Canadian experience

In 1985, the Privy Council for Canada established the Deschenes Commission of Inquiry on War Criminals to investigate whether any war criminals resided in Canada and how they could be brought to justice. Specifically, the Commission was established:

> to conduct such investigations regarding alleged war criminals in Canada, including whether any such persons are now resident in Canada and when and how they obtained entry to Canada as in the opinion of the Commissioner are necessary in order to enable him to report to the Governor in Council his recommendations and advice relating to what further action might be taken in Canada to bring to justice such alleged war criminals who might be residing within Canada, including recommendations as to what legal means are now available to bring to justice any such persons in Canada or whether and what legislation might be adopted by the Parliament of Canada to ensure that war criminals are brought to justice and made to answer for their crimes.[301]

299 *See supra* Section 5.

300 *See also* Ellen Lutz and Kathryn Sikkink, *The Justice Cascade: The Evolution and Impact of Foreign Human Rights Trials in Latin America*, 2 CHI. J. INT'L L. 1 (2001); Human Rights Committee, International Law Association (British Branch), EUR. HUM. RTS. L. REV. 129 (2001). *See also* Brigitte Stern, *International Decision: In re Javor; In re Munyeshyaka*, 93 AM. J. INT'L L. 525 (1999).

301 Order in Council, PC-1985-348, Feb. 5, 1985 (Ca.).

On December 30, 1986, the Deschenes Commission released its report.[302] The Commission investigated 774 people suspected of being war criminals.[303] After conducting extensive investigations, the Commission identified approximately 20 individuals against whom revocation of citizenship and deportation proceedings or criminal prosecution should be commenced. It also identified approximately 200 other cases where further investigations were warranted. In addition, the Deschenes Commission recommended amending the Canadian criminal code to prosecute war criminals.

In response to the findings of the Deschenes Commission, Canada enacted legislation to establish criminal liability for anyone who had committed war crimes or crimes against humanity regardless of where such acts occurred. The Canadian Criminal Code was amended to read:

> [E]very person who, either before or after the coming into
> force of this subsection, commits an act or omission
> outside Canada that constitutes a war crime or a crime
> against humanity and that, if committed in Canada, would
> constitute an offense against the laws of Canada in force
> at the time of the act or omission shall be deemed to
> commit that act or omission in Canada at that time if,
>> (a) at the time of the act or omission,
>>> (i) that person is a Canadian citizen or is
>>> employed by Canada in a civilian or military
>>> capacity,
>>> (ii) that person is a citizen of, or is employed in a
>>> civilian or military capacity by, a state that is
>>> engaged in an armed conflict against Canada, or
>>> (iii) the victim of the act or omission is a Canadian
>>> citizen or a citizen of a state that is allied with
>>> Canada in an armed conflict; or
>> (b) at the time of the act or omission, Canada could,
>> in conformity with international law, exercise juris-
>> diction over the person with respect to the act or

---

302 Commission of Inquiry on War Criminals (1986).

303 For overview of how Nazi war criminals first entered Canada, see Howard Margolian, Unauthorized Entry: The Truth About Nazi War Criminals in Canada 1946–1956 (2000). *See also* Patrick Brode, Casual Slaughters and Accidental Judgments: Canadian War Crimes Prosecutions, 1944–1948 (1997).

omission on the basis of the person's presence in
Canada and, subsequent to the time of the act or
omission, the person is present in Canada.[304]

The definition of "crimes against humanity" provided by the
statute was quite broad and was not limited to acts that took place
during war.[305] According to the Canadian Ministry of Justice, "[t]he
law is generic and refers to all war criminals around the world.
Specific cases that . . . are brought to our attention, regardless of
where they arise, [will be given] serious attention."[306]

In one of the first prosecutions under this legislation, Imre
Finta was charged with war crimes and crimes against humanity
for his purported actions against Hungarian Jews during World
War II. Finta was alleged to have been a senior officer at a
detention camp in Hungary, where he was said to have been
responsible for the detention, confinement, and eventual death of
thousands of Jews. After an eight-month trial, Finta was acquitted
on all counts. The Canadian government then appealed numerous
rulings by the trial court to the Ontario Court of Appeal, which
upheld the acquittal.[307] The case was then appealed to the
Supreme Court of Canada. In *Regina v. Finta*, the Supreme Court of
Canada narrowly affirmed the lower court rulings.[308] The Supreme
Court's ruling was significant because it made it easier for individuals to raise a defense based upon superior orders.[309]

Partly in response to the *Finta* ruling, the Canadian government altered its policy of seeking criminal prosecution of alleged

304 Act to Amend the Criminal Code, ch. 37, 1987 Can. Stat. 1107 (Ca.).

305 "Crimes against humanity" is defined as "murder, extermination, enslavement,
deportation, persecution or any other inhumane act or omission that is committed against
any civilian population or any identifiable group of persons, whether or not it constitutes a
contravention of the law in force at the time and in the place of its commission, and that, at
that time and in that place, constitutes a contravention of customary international law or
conventional international law or is criminal according to the general principles of law
recognized by the community of nations." R.S.C. 1985, c. C-46, s.7, at 3.76 (Ca.).

306 Edmonton Journal, Sept. 7, 1988. *But see* L.C. Green, *Canadian Law, War Crimes and
Crimes Against Humanity*, 59 BRIT. Y.B. INT'L L. 217, 229 (1988).

307 In Canada, the government can appeal jury acquittals. Appeals courts have the authority
to set aside an acquittal and order a new trial. R.S.C., ch. C-46, §686(4) (1985) (Ca.).

308 Regina v. Finta, [1994] 1 S.C.R. 701.

309 *See generally* Irwin Cotler, *International Decision: Regina v. Finta*, 90 AM. J. INT'L L. 460
(1996).

war criminals. Instead, it decided to focus on immigration restrictions, including denaturalization and deportation of suspected war criminals. According to the Canadian government,

> The decision of the Supreme Court of Canada in *R. v. Finta* is particularly relevant here. In that case, the Court established a higher standard of proof for the prosecution of war crimes and crimes against humanity than is recognized at international law. For the World War II cases, this decision has made prosecution of these crimes much more difficult and less likely.[310]

In July 1998, the Canadian government issued a public report outlining its revised program with respect to war crimes and crimes against humanity. It announced the allocation of $46.8 million over the next three years to pursue its policy "to bring to justice those persons in Canada responsible for war crimes, crimes against humanity and other reprehensible acts in times of war, regardless of when those acts occurred."[311] The Canadian War Crimes Program addresses both war crimes and crimes against humanity committed at any time. Three agencies participate in this program: the Department of Citizenship and Immigration, the Department of Justice, and the Royal Canadian Mounted Police.

In its 2001 Annual Report on the War Crimes Program, the Government of Canada states that "Canada will not become a safe haven for those individuals who have committed war crimes, crimes against humanity or any other reprehensible act during times of conflict."[312] The Report indicates that several remedies are available to deal with war crimes and crimes against humanity.

> The decision to use one or more of these mechanisms is based on a number of factors. These factors include: the different requirements of the courts in criminal and immigration/refugee cases to substantiate and verify

310 Canadian Department of Justice, Press Release, Federal Government Announces WWII Crimes Strategy, and Background Paper, The Investigation of War Crimes in Canada (Jan. 31, 1995), at 8.

311 GOVERNMENT OF CANADA, PUBLIC REPORT: CANADA'S WAR CRIMES PROGRAM 2 (1998).

312 GOVERNMENT OF CANADA, CANADA'S WAR CRIMES PROGRAM: ANNUAL REPORT (2001) [hereinafter "CANADA'S 2001 ANNUAL REPORT"].

evidence; an appropriate allocation of resources in the
circumstances to provide a balanced approach; and
Canada's obligations under international law. These
remedies are:

- criminal prosecution in Canada;
- extradition to a foreign government;
- surrender to an international tribunal;
- revocation of citizenship and deportation;
- denial of visa to persons outside of Canada;
- denial of access (exclusion) to the refugee
  determination system; and,
- inquiry and removal from Canada under the
  Immigration Act.[313]

According to the 2001 Annual Report, Canada refused entry to
644 individuals from April 1, 1999 to March 31, 2000 for war crimes-
related allegations.[314] This constitutes a 14% increase from the
previous year. In addition, 53 individuals were denied refugee
status because of war crimes allegations. This constitutes a 51%
increase from the previous year. With respect to removal proceedings, 42 individuals were removed from Canada because of
war crimes allegations, representing a 10% increase. To date, a
total of 1,566 persons have been refused admission to Canada for
war crimes or crimes against humanity, and 187 persons have been
removed from Canada. In describing the accomplishments of its
War Crimes Program, the Government of Canada has indicated:

Victims of wars, oppression and human rights violations
will continue to flee to countries such as Canada in order
to seek refugee status. Canada is proud of its record in
granting protection to refugees. Unfortunately, among
these victims often come their persecutors, some of
whom are war criminals or perpetrators of crimes against
humanity. The challenge to be met by Canada and other
like-minded countries is to ensure that the right balance
is met in designing systems and processes to protect the
legitimate refugee while ensuring that persons who have

313 *Id.*
314 *Id.*

committed war crimes, crimes against humanity and other
reprehensible acts are not only refused protection, but
are dealt with the full force of the law.[315]

Despite these efforts by the Canadian government, com-
mentators have criticized the manner in which Canada has
implemented its modern war crimes program. By focusing
primarily on immigration restrictions, Canada has overlooked
its obligation to prosecute suspected terrorists. As noted by
one commentator, "[d]eportation is relocation of the criminal
but not punishment of the crime. A person who comes to
Canada and then is told to move on has received a temporary
haven and then a temporary inconvenience."[316] Indeed,
Canada has chosen to remove numerous individuals who
were apparently eligible for prosecution under the Convention
against Torture.[317]

In response to these criticisms, the Canadian Government
adopted legislation in 2000 to amend various provisions of the
Criminal Code and the Immigration Act.[318] The Crimes Against
Humanity and War Crimes Act establishes new criminal offenses
of genocide, crimes against humanity, war crimes, and breach of
responsibility by military and civilian leaders. It also implements
Canada's obligations under the Rome Statute of the International
Criminal Court.[319]

315 GOVERNMENT OF CANADA, CANADA'S WAR CRIMES PROGRAM: ANNUAL REPORT 22 (2000)
[hereinafter "CANADA'S 2000 ANNUAL REPORT"].

316 David Matas, Remarks at the Centre for Refugee Studies (Feb. 29, 2000).

317 See CANADA'S 2001 ANNUAL REPORT, supra, at passim. See also Claire I. Farid, A Primer on
Citizenship Revocation for WWII Collaboration: The 1998–1999 Federal Court Term, 38
ALBERTA L. REV. 415 (2000); William Schabas, International Decision: Mugesera v. Minister of
Citizenship and Immigration, 93 AM. J. INT'L L. 529 (1999).

318 Bill C-19: Crimes against Humanity and War Crimes Act (2000) (Ca.).

319 The law also codifies various defenses to prosecution, including double jeopardy,
obedience to internal law, and superior orders. With respect to the superior orders
defense, the law provides that persons cannot base their defense on a belief that the
order was lawful if that belief was based on information that encouraged, was likely to
encourage, or attempted to justify inhumane acts against a civilian population or identifiable group of persons. This provision was added to addresses the Canadian Supreme Court's
ruling in the Finta case, which would allow an individual to rely on propaganda as the basis
for a defense of honest but mistaken belief in the lawfulness of superior orders. See David
Goetz, Bill C-19: Crimes against Humanity and War Crimes Act (2000).

The Belgian experience

In 1993, Belgium adopted legislation to establish universal juris-diction for certain violations of international law. The "Act Concerning the Punishment of Grave Breaches of the 1949 Geneva Conventions and Protocols I and II" established criminal liability for grave breaches that cause injury or damage to persons protected by the 1949 Geneva Conventions and by Protocols I and II, both of which had been adopted by Belgium.[320]

In 1996, the Belgian Senate convened a colloquium to address whether Belgium should extend the principles of the 1993 Act to include other violations of international law, including genocide and crimes against humanity.[321] Subsequent developments, including the adoption of the Rome Statute and the Pinochet prosecution, further influenced Belgian legislative efforts.[322] In 1999, Belgium promulgated the "Act Concerning the Punishment of Grave Breaches of International Humanitarian Law."[323] The 1999 Act incorporates the provisions of the 1993 Act and adds that genocide and crimes against humanity constitute crimes under international law and may be punished. Significantly, Article 7 provides that "[t]he Belgian courts shall be competent to deal with breaches provided for in the present Act, irrespective of where such breaches have been committed."[324] The Act restricts available defenses. Immunity attributed to official capacity does not preclude prosecution.[325] Superior orders is not a valid defense where the order could clearly result in the commission of a crime.[326] Other statutory limitations are also

---

320 Loi du 16 juin 1993 relative á la répression des infractions graves aux Conventions internationales de Genève du 12 août 1949 et aux Protocols I et II du 8 juin 1977, additionnels à ces Conventions (Aug. 5, 1993) (Be.).

321 Luc Reydams, Universal Criminal Jurisdiction: The Belgian State of Affairs, 11 CRIM. L.F. 183, 190 (2000).

322 Id. at 194.

323 Loi relative à la répression des violations graves du droit international humanitaire (March 23, 1999) (Be.). See also Belgium: Act Concerning the Punishment of Grave Breaches of International Humanitarian Law, 38 I.L.M. 918 (1999).

324 Loi relative à la répression des violations graves du droit international humanitaire, supra, at art. 7.

325 Id. at art. 5(3).

326 Id. at art. 5(2).

inapplicable.[327] Punishment for violations of the Act ranges from 10 years' imprisonment to life imprisonment.[328]

Belgium has initiated several proceedings pursuant to this legislation. In November 1998, for example, a criminal complaint was filed against Augusto Pinochet, who was then under detention in the United Kingdom.[329] The complaint, filed pursuant to the 1993 law, alleged that Pinochet had committed grave breaches of the Geneva Conventions during his presidency. The investigating magistrate charged with the case reviewed several issues, including the validity of the universal jurisdiction provisions of Belgian law and the immunity of a former head of state. The investigating magistrate upheld the validity of the universal jurisdiction provisions. He also found that acts of torture, murder and hostage-taking could not be considered official acts of a head of state and, therefore, Pinochet could not be immune from prosecution.

Proceedings involving human rights abuses in Rwanda have also been prosecuted in Belgium. In April 2001, four Rwandan nationals were brought to trial in Belgium on charges of war crimes allegedly committed in Rwanda in 1994.[330] On June 8, 2001, the four defendants were found guilty of most of the 55 counts. They received prison sentences ranging from 12 years to 20 years.[331] Several other criminal complaints based upon the universal jurisdiction provisions of Belgian law are pending.[332]

Recent challenges have been raised against the Belgian legislation. At the national level, Belgian legislators are now considering limiting the scope of the legislation so that it excludes foreign government leaders.[333] Such immunity would exist while

327 *Id.* at art. 6.

328 *Id.* at art. 2.

329 *See generally* Luc Reydams, *International Decision: Belgian Tribunal of First Instance of Brussels,* 93 AM. J. INT'L L. 700 (2000).

330 *See generally* Barry James, *A Conflicted Belgium Examines Its Colonial Past in Genocide Trial,* INT'L HERALD TRIB., Apr. 25, 2001, at 5.

331 Peter Ford, *Belgium Pursues Justice Without Borders,* CHRISTIAN SCI. MONITOR, June 11, 2001, at 1.

332 Reydams, Universal Criminal Jurisdiction, *supra,* at 213.

333 Marlise Simons, *Human Rights Cases Begin to Flood Into Belgian Courts,* NEW YORK TIMES, Dec. 27, 2001, at A8; Anton La Guardia, *West Accused of Double Standard,* THE DAILY TELEGRAPH (LONDON), July 13, 2001, at 20.

the foreign government official was in office.[334] At the inter-national level, the Democratic Republic of the Congo ("DRC") instituted proceedings in the International Court of Justice against Belgium in October 2000 challenging these provisions of Belgian law.[335] According to the DRC, a Belgian investigating judge had issued an international arrest warrant against the DRC Minister of Foreign Affairs, seeking his provisional detention pending a request for extradition for alleged violations of international humanitarian law. The DRC argued that the Belgian arrest warrant and the underlying Belgian statutory provisions violated international law. In particular, the DRC argued that the actions of Belgium in setting forth universal jurisdiction violated the principle of sovereign equality set forth in the United Nations Charter. On February 14, 2002, the International Court of Justice ruled that an arrest warrant for crimes under international law could not be issued against a minister of foreign affairs while in office.

The Swiss experience

Switzerland has established universal jurisdiction for violations of international human rights law in its Penal Code and Military Penal Code. Article 6*bis* of the Swiss Penal Code provides that the Code is applicable to crimes committed abroad that Switzer-land is obligated to prosecute under an international agreement, provided that the act is also punishable in the state where it was committed, and the suspect is present in Switzerland and is not extradited.[336] However, Article 6*bis* provides that the suspect may not be prosecuted if he or she was acquitted in the state where the acts were committed or if he or she has already been punished for the acts. According to the Swiss

---

334 *See* Vivienne Walt, *A Continent's Targets*, NEWSDAY, July 16, 2001, at A4; *Belgium Considers Immunity for Foreign Leaders*, AGENCE FRANCE PRESSE, July 12, 2001; Herb Keinon, *Belgium Embarrassed By Anti-Sharon Suits*, JERUSALEM POST, July 6, 2001.

335 Application Instituting Proceedings (Democratic Republic of the Congo v. Belgium) (Oct. 17, 2000). *See also* Case Concerning the Arrest Warrant of 11 April 2000 (Democratic Republic of the Congo v. Belgium) (Feb. 14, 2002) (http://www.icj-cij.org).

336 Code pénal suisse 6bis (Sw.).

government, this provision establishes jurisdiction for acts of torture.[337] In addition, Article 109 of the Swiss Military Penal Code establishes criminal liability for anyone who acts contrary to the provisions of international agreements on the conduct of war or with respect to the laws and customs of war.[338] Article 108 gives military tribunals jurisdiction over these violations, whether they were committed during an international or non-international armed conflict.[339]

Several prosecutions have been pursued under the Swiss universal jurisdiction regime. In February 1997, Goran Grabez was indicted by a Swiss military prosecutor for violations of the laws and customs of war in Bosnia-Herzegovina. The indictment alleged that Grabez participated in atrocities at the Omarska and Keraterm detention camps in Bosnia-Herzegovina. Grabez was tried before a Swiss military tribunal in July 1997.[340] While the military tribunal determined that the provisions of the Geneva Conventions applied to the conflict in Bosnia-Herzegovina, it acquitted Grabez because the prosecution had failed to prove his guilt beyond a reasonable doubt.[341]

In July 1998, Fulgence Niyonteze, former mayor of Mushubati, Rwanda, was charged with genocide, crimes against humanity, and war crimes.[342] Prior to Niyonteze's trial, a Swiss military tribunal determined that he could not be prosecuted for genocide or crimes against humanity because the Swiss law did not provide jurisdiction for these offenses. Accordingly, Niyonteze was only prosecuted for war crimes. In May 1999, Niyonteze was convicted of war crimes by the military tribunal. On appeal, his conviction was confirmed although his original sentence of life imprisonment was reduced to 14 years.[343]

---

337 Initial Report of Switzerland to the U.N. Committee against Torture, U.N. Doc. CAT/C/5/Add.17, at 8 (1989).

338 Code pénal militaire 109 (Sw.).

339 *Id.* at art. 108.

340 Andreas R. Ziegler, *International Decision: In Re G.*, 92 AM. J. INT'L L. 78 (1999).

341 The defendant was also awarded 100,000 Swiss francs for damages, an amount subsequently reduced to 20,000 Swiss francs on appeal.

342 Niyonteze arrived in Switzerland in October 1994, when he applied for asylum. He was arrested in August 1996. *Rwandan Suspected of War Crimes to Go on Trial in April*, AGENCE FRANCE PRESSE, Feb. 1, 1999.

343 *Switzerland Confirms Former Rwandan Mayor's War Crimes Sentence*, AGENCE FRANCE PRESSE, April 27, 2001; *Swiss Convict Rwandan Official in Massacre*, WASHINGTON POST, May 1, 1999, at A10.

The Spanish experience

Article 23(4) of the Spanish Organic Law of Judicial Power establishes criminal jurisdiction for such crimes as genocide, terrorism, piracy, aircraft hijacking, or "any other [crime] which according to international treaties or conventions must be prosecuted in Spain" regardless of where such actions were committed.[344] Similarly, Title XXIV of the Spanish Penal Code establishes liability for crimes committed against the international community. Chapter I establishes criminal liability for causing the death or injury of a foreign head of state or any other internationally protected person.[345] Chapter II imposes criminal liability for anyone who, "with the objective of total or partial destruction of a national, ethnic, racial or religious group," commits the following acts: killing of some of its members; sexual assault on some of its members; submission of the group or any of its individual members to living conditions which put their lives in danger or seriously endanger their health; carrying out forced relocation of the group or its members, or adoption of any measure which tends to impede its regeneration or reproduction; or any forced movement of individuals of one group from another.[346] Finally, Chapter III imposes criminal liability for anyone who mistreats or places in danger the health, safety, or well-being of persons specially protected in case of armed conflict.[347]

The Spanish legal system also provides a role for Spanish citizens and foreigners in the prosecution of criminal actions. Article 125 of the Spanish Constitution allows all Spanish citizens to participate in criminal proceedings.[348] Article 101 of the Code of Criminal Procedure provides that all Spanish citizens may file an *acción popular,* or popular action, in

---

344 LEY ORGANICA DEL PODER JUDICIAL art. 23 (Sp.).

345 CÓDIGO PENAL art. 605 (Sp.).

346 *Id.* at art. 607.

347 *Id.* at art. 608.

348 CONSTITUCIÓN ESPAÑOL art. 125 (Sp.).

criminal proceedings.[349] Once the complaint is filed and accepted by the court, the person initiating the complaint becomes a party to the criminal proceedings.[350] Additionally, Article 270 of the Code of Criminal Procedure provides that any foreigners who were injured by the violation, as well as all Spanish citizens (regardless of whether they were injured by the violation), may file a similar action.[351]

In addition, Spanish law provides that every person who is criminally liable may also be responsible for civil damages.[352] Civil liability includes restitution and compensation for any damages. Civil remedies may be pursued by either the victim or the public prosecutor if the victim has not reserved the right to pursue civil damages.[353]

Implementation of these provisions has been most evident in two cases, one involving former Argentine military officers, and the other involving former Chilean military officers, including Augusto Pinochet.[354] Criminal charges against Pinochet were originally filed in July 1996 before the *Audiencia Nacional*, which has jurisdiction over crimes not committed in Spanish territory. The complaint charged Pinochet with terrorism, torture, murder, genocide, and crimes against humanity. Prosecuting magistrates confirmed their jurisdiction over these cases in several preliminary rulings. In early October 1998, Spanish magistrate Baltazar Garzón was notified that Pinochet was in England. He immediately issued a provisional arrest

---

349 LEY DE ENJUICIAMIENTO CRIMINAL art. 101 (Sp.).

350 ELEMA MERINO-BLANCO, THE SPANISH LEGAL SYSTEM 162 (1996).

351 LEY DE ENJUICIAMIENTO CRIMINAL, *supra*, at art. 270.

352 *Id.* at art. 100.

353 *Id.* at art. 108.

354 *See generally* THE PINOCHET PAPERS: THE CASE OF AUGUSTO PINOCHET IN SPAIN AND BRITAIN (Reed Brody & Michael Ratner eds., 2000); THE PINOCHET CASE: A LEGAL AND CONSTITUTIONAL HISTORY (Diana Woodhouse ed., 2000); Christine Chinkin, *International Decision: R v. Bow Street Metropolitan Stipendiary Magistrate*, 93 AM. J. INT'L L. 703 (1999); Nehal Bhuta, *Justice Without Borders? Prosecuting General Pinochet*, 12 MELBOURNE U. L. REV. 499 (1999); Maria del Carmen Marquez Carrasco & Joaquin Alcaide Fernandez, *International Decision: In re Pinochet*, 93 AM. J. INT'L L. 690 (1999); Neil Boister & Richard Burchill, *The Pinochet Precedent: Don't Leave Home Without It*, 10 CRIM. L.F. 405 (1999) .

warrant and submitted it to Scotland Yard for execution. On October 16, 1998, British authorities served Pinochet with the arrest warrant.[355] While the English proceedings were developing, the *Audiencia Nacional*, sitting *en banc*, unanimously upheld Spanish jurisdiction in the Argentine and Chilean cases. The court indicated that Spain had jurisdiction over the alleged crimes of genocide and terrorism committed abroad by foreign nationals. Furthermore, it found jurisdiction for the crime of torture because it was a constituent part of the broader crime of genocide.

On March 24, 1999, the House of Lords issued its own groundbreaking ruling in the Pinochet case.[356] The majority of Law Lords concluded that a former head of state could not claim immunity for acts of torture.[357] The Law Lords differed, however, in their reasoning, which recognized the relevance of both the Convention against Torture and customary international law. In his own opinion, Lord Millett was emphatic about restricting head of state immunity to former heads of state for acts of torture. "International law cannot be supposed to have established a crime having the character of a *jus cogens* and at the same time to have provided an immunity which is co-extensive with the obligation it seeks to impose."[358]

On March 2, 2000, British Secretary of State Jack Straw determined that Pinochet was not mentally fit to stand trial and, therefore, he would not be extradited to Spain. Although the United Kingdom returned Pinochet to Chile, the Pinochet case reinforces

---

355 During the British proceedings, the Committee against Torture issued the following statement:

> The Committee finally recommends that in the case of Senator Pinochet of Chile, the matter be referred to the office of the public prosecutor, with a view to examining the feasibility of and if appropriate initiating criminal proceedings in England, in the event that the decision is made not to extradite him. This would satisfy the State party's obligations under articles 4 and 7 of the Convention and article 27 of the Vienna Convention on the Law of Treaties 1969.

U.N. Doc. CAT/C/SR.360. (Nov. 23, 1998).

356 A prior ruling by the House of Lords in the Pinochet case was withdrawn due to a potential conflict of interest between one of the Law Lords and Amnesty International, which had intervened in the proceedings.

357 R v. Bow Street Metropolitan Stipendiary Magistrate, *ex parte* Pinochet Ugarte (Amnesty International and others intervening) (No. 3), 2 All E.R. 97 (H.L. 1999).

358 *Id.* at 179 (Lord Millett).

state practice concerning universal jurisdiction over crimes under international law. It also acted as a catalyst for action in Chile, reinforcing efforts by Chilean judges and prosecutors to pursue criminal suits against Pinochet.[359]

*****

A cursory review of recent cases reveals that a number of countries have responded to human rights abuses committed abroad by taking steps to ensure that perpetrators who are present in their territory are brought to justice.[360]

- In February 2001, a German court dismissed the appeal of Maxim Sokolovic, who was convicted in November 1999 of complicity in genocide for acts committed in Osmaci, Bosnia.[361] He is currently serving a nine-year sentence in Germany.[362]
- In November 2000, Denmark surrendered former Rwandan Army Captain Innocent Sagahutu to the International Criminal Tribunal for Rwanda. Sagahutu was accused of genocide and crimes against humanity. He subsequently pled innocent to the charges.[363]
- In November 1999, Spanish judge Baltasar Garzón initiated proceedings against former Argentine military officer Miguel Angel Cavallo, who was accused of the torture and murder of Spanish citizens during Argentina's Dirty War.[364] On August 24, 2000, the Mexican government arrested the suspect.[365] In

---

359 See generally Sebastian Rotella & Eva Vergara, Pinochet Loses Immunity, But a Trial is Unlikely, LOS ANGELES TIMES, Aug. 9, 2000, at A1; Anthony Faiola, Chile Strips Pinochet of Immunity From Trial, INT'L HERALD TRIB., Aug. 9, 2000, at 1.

360 See also INTERNATIONAL LAW ASSOCIATION, FINAL REPORT ON THE EXERCISE OF UNIVERSAL JURISDICTION IN RESPECT OF GROSS HUMAN RIGHTS OFFENCES 28 (2000); REDRESS, UNIVERSAL JURISDICTION IN EUROPE (1999).

361 German Court Rejects Appeal of Serb Convicted of Genocide, AGENCE FRANCE PRESSE, Feb. 29, 2001.

362 Serb Given Nine-Year Prison Term for Genocide, AGENCE FRANCE PRESSE, Nov. 29, 1999.

363 Former Rwandan Army Captain Pleads Not Guilty to Genocide, Crimes against Humanity, AFRICA NEWS, Nov. 29, 2000.

364 Juan E. Mendez & Salvador Tinajero-Esquivel, The Cavallo Case: A New Test for Universal Jurisdiction, 8 HUM. RTS. BRIEF 5 (2001); Alan Zarembo, The Search for Serpico, NEWSWEEK, Sept. 18, 2000, at 29; Tim Weiner & Ginger Thompson, Wide Net in Argentine Torture Case, NEW YORK TIMES, Sept. 11, 2000, at A6.

365 James F. Smith, Argentine in Mexico Linked to 'Dirty War,' LOS ANGELES TIMES, August 25, 2000, at A4.

January 2001, the Mexican government announced it would extradite the suspect to Spain. The suspect has appealed these rulings.

• In April 1999, the German Federal Supreme Court upheld a lower court's jurisdiction to prosecute Nikola Jorgic, a Serbian national, for genocide based on his role in ethnic cleansing that occurred in Bosnia during the Yugoslav conflict.[366] In September 1997, Jorgic was convicted of genocide and murder. He is currently serving a life sentence in Germany.[367]

• In May 1997, Novislav Djajic was convicted by a German court for being an accessory to the murder of 14 Muslims in Eastern Bosnia during the Yugoslav conflict. He was sentenced in 1997 to a five-year term in Germany.[368]

• On November 25, 1994, a Bosnian Serb, Refik Saric, was convicted of war crimes by a Danish court.[369] The sentence was confirmed on appeal by the Danish Supreme Court. Saric was sentenced to eight years' imprisonment.

*****

The following cases involve alleged human rights abusers who have thus far eluded punishment despite efforts to try them in other countries.[370] These cases underscore the need for stronger national programs and international cooperation. Efforts to prosecute these crimes in national courts cannot succeed in the absence of international cooperation.

---

366 Bundesgerichtshof, Urteil vom 30 April 1999—3 StR 215/98; *German Federal Supreme Court Upholds Its Jurisdiction to Prosecute Serb National for Genocide Based on His Role in "Ethnic Cleansing" That Occurred in Bosnia and Herzegovina*, 5 INT'L L. UPDATE 52 (May 1999).

367 *Serb Joins List of Bosnia War Crimes Convictions*, AGENCE FRANCE PRESSE, Nov. 29, 1999.

368 Peter Ford, *Answering for Rights Crimes*, CHRISTIAN SCI. MONITOR, Oct. 8, 1999, at 1; Christoph J. M. Safferling, *International Decision: Public Prosecutor v. Djajic*, 92 AM. J. INT'L L. 528 (1998).

369 Ford *supra*, at 1.

370 On several occasions, individuals suspected of having committed human rights abuses have been acquitted in criminal proceedings. On May 31, 1995, for example, a Bosnian Serb, Dusko Cvjetkovic was acquitted of genocide and murder by an Austrian district court. In earlier proceedings, the Austrian Supreme Court had determined that Austrian courts had jurisdiction over such cases. *See* Axel Marschik, *The Politics of Prosecution: European National Approaches to War Crimes, in* THE LAW OF WAR CRIMES 65 (Timothy L.J. McCormack & Gerry J. Simpson eds., 1997).

- In April 2001, an Argentine judge requested the arrest of former Paraguayan leader Alfredo Stroessner, who is living in Brazil.[371] A criminal complaint has been filed in Paraguay charging Stroessner with human rights abuses, including torture and murder.[372] In August 2000, a congressional commission in Brazil filed a petition requesting that Stroessner be indicted.[373]

- In December 2000, an Italian court found former Argentine General Guillermo Suarez Mason guilty for his role in the disappearance and murder of Italian citizens in Argentina. Suarez Mason was sentenced *in absentia* to life imprisonment. Several other Argentine officers were also sentenced.[374]

- In February 2000, former Chadian President Hissene Habré was detained in Senegal on charges of torture and crimes against humanity allegedly committed during his administration. On several occasions, however, the newly elected government of Abdoulaye Wade intervened in the criminal proceedings. In March 2001, the charges against Habré were dropped, and he was released.[375] Numerous efforts have been made to renew the proceedings against Habré.[376] In April 2001, the Committee against Torture called upon the Senegalese government to prevent Habré from leaving the country.[377]

- In July 1999, a Mauritanian military official, Ely Ould Dah, was arrested in France and charged with acts of torture.[378] Upon

371 *Argentine Judge Requests Arrest of former Paraguayan Dictator Stroessner,* AGENCE FRANCE PRESSE, April 15, 2001.

372 *New Torture and Homicide Charges Filed Against Stroessner,* EFE NEWS SERVICE, April 24, 2001.

373 Anthony Faiola, *'Pinochet Effect' Exposes Once-Untouchable Ex-Dictators,* INT'L HERALD TRIB., Aug. 7, 2000, at 9.

374 Philip Willan, *Italy to Try South American Generals,* THE GUARDIAN, March 17, 2001, at 21. Amnesty International believes that *in absentia* trials are inconsistent with the right to be tried in one's presence.

375 David Bosco, *Dictators in the Dock,* AM. PROSPECT, Aug. 14, 2000, at 26; *Justice Denied in Senegal,* NEW YORK TIMES, July 21, 2000, at A18.

376 *See generally* Norimitsu Onishi, *He Bore Up Under Torture, Now He Bears Witness,* NEW YORK TIMES, March 31, 2001, at A3.

377 *UN Committee Seeks to Prevent Habré from Leaving Senegal,* AGENCE FRANCE PRESSE, April 23, 2001.

378 Ford *supra,* at 1.

being released on bail in April 2000, Ould Dah immediately fled the country and returned to Mauritania.

Non-governmental organizations such as Amnesty International, the Center for Constitutional Rights, the Center for Justice & Accountability, *Fédération internationale des ligues des droits de l'homme*, Human Rights Watch, the International Commission of Jurists, the Lawyers Committee for Human Rights, and Redress have sought to remedy the twofold problem of impunity abroad and inaction at home.[379] They have advocated for greater national and international efforts to combat impunity. They have also played an important role in several prominent cases, including the Pinochet and Habré cases.

---

379 *See* HUMAN RIGHTS WATCH, THE PINOCHET PRECEDENT: HOW VICTIMS CAN PURSUE HUMAN RIGHTS CRIMINALS ABROAD (2000); REDRESS, CHALLENGING IMPUNITY FOR TORTURE: A MANUAL FOR BRINGING CRIMINAL AND CIVIL PROCEEDINGS IN ENGLAND AND WALES FOR TORTURE COMMITTED ABROAD (2000); AMNESTY INTERNATIONAL, UNITED KINGDOM: UNIVERSAL JURISDICTION AND ABSENCE OF IMMUNITY FOR CRIMES AGAINST HUMANITY (1999); INTERNATIONAL COUNCIL ON HUMAN RIGHTS POLICY, HARD CASES: BRINGING HUMAN RIGHTS VIOLATORS TO JUSTICE ABROAD (1999).

9: Policy recommendations

"Justice is truth in action."

—Jozias van Aartsen[380]

  The Netherlands Minister of Foreign Affairs, quoting
  Benjamin Disraeli at a conference on implementing
  the International Criminal Court

The situation of survivors living side by side with torturers in the United States reveals significant limitations in current U.S. policy. Accordingly, Amnesty International USA proposes the following recommendations to ensure the United States is not a safe haven for human rights abusers.[381]

Words of caution

Throughout the implementation of these recommendations, all relevant human rights principles should be respected. The purpose of these recommendations is not to make it more difficult for legitimate immigrants and refugees to enter and remain in the United States. The United States has benefited greatly from allowing immigrants to enter the country. It also has a responsibility under national and international law to protect individuals fleeing war and persecution. Rather, the purpose of these recommendations is quite specific—to combat impunity.

To accuse an individual of torture is a serious charge.[382] It can have profound personal implications on the suspect. It can affect family and social relations. It can also lead to civil and criminal liability. Accordingly, allegations of torture should be treated with caution and circumspection.

Individuals can only be held responsible for acts of torture if the material elements of the acts were committed with intent

---

380 *Justice is Truth in Action*, Opening Remarks by Jozias van Aartsen, Minister of Foreign Affairs, at the Conference "Implementing the ICC," Peace Palace, The Hague (December 19, 2001).

381 These recommendations apply to all acts of torture, including attempts to commit torture as well as acts that constitute complicity or participation in torture.

382 *See generally* AMNESTY INTERNATIONAL, TORTURE IN THE EIGHTIES 90-94 (1984).

and knowledge.[383] A person has the "intent" to commit torture if he or she means to engage in the conduct or means to cause that consequence or is aware that it will occur in the ordinary course of events. A person has "knowledge" where he or she is aware that a circumstance exists or a consequence will occur in the ordinary course of events. Accordingly, persons who suffer from mental disabilities or other impairments that significantly influence their capacity to appreciate the unlawfulness or nature of their conduct should not be held responsible for their actions.[384] Similarly, persons under the age of 18 should be dealt with in a manner that takes into account their age and situation.[385]

Individuals with command responsibility, whether military or political, should be held responsible for the acts of subordinates in appropriate circumstances.[386] Indeed, the U.S. Senate's understanding of Article 1 of the Convention against Torture makes clear that liability extends to a public official who has awareness of activity constituting torture and thereafter breaches "his legal responsibility to intervene to prevent such activity."[387]

383 According to the Rome Statute, a person shall be criminally responsible and liable for punishment for a crime within the jurisdiction of the Court only if the material elements are committed with intent and knowledge. Rome Statute of the International Criminal Court, July 17, 1998, art. 30, U.N. Doc. A/CONF. 183/9 [hereinafter "Rome Statute"]. A person has "intent" where: (a) in relation to conduct, that person means to engage in the conduct; (b) in relation to a consequence, that person means to cause that consequence or is aware that it will occur in the ordinary course of events. "Knowledge" means awareness that a circumstance exists or a consequence will occur in the ordinary course of events. *Id.*

384 Rome Statute, *supra*, at art. 30. *See generally* Peter Krug, *The Emerging Mental Incapacity Defense in International Criminal Law: Some Initial Questions of Implementation*, 94 AM. J. INT'L L. 317 (2000).

385 Rome Statute, *supra*, at art. 26. *See also* Convention on the Rights of the Child, Nov. 20, 1989, art. 40, 1577 U.N.T.S. 3.

386 *See* Rome Statute, *supra*, at art. 28. Under international law, a military commander or person effectively acting as a military commander may be criminally responsible for crimes committed by forces under his or her effective command and control, or effective authority and control as the case may be, as a result of his or her failure to exercise control properly over such forces. *See* In re Yamashita, 327 U.S. 1 (1946). *See generally* Danesh Sarooshi, *Command Responsibility and the Blaskic Case* 50 INT'L & COMP. L.Q. 452 (2001); Greg R. Vetter, *Command Responsibility of Non-Military Superiors in the International Criminal Court*, 25 YALE J. INT'L L. 89 (2000); Andrew D. Mitchell, *Failure to Halt, Prevent or Punish: The Doctrine of Command Responsibility for War Crimes*, 22 SYDNEY L. REV. 381 (2000); L.C. Green, *Command Responsibility in International Humanitarian Law*, 5 TRANSNAT'L L. & CONTEMP. PROBS. 319 (1995).

387 The Initial Report of the United States to the Committee against Torture indicates that the purpose of the Senate understanding is "to make it clear that both actual knowledge and 'willful blindness' fall within the definition of 'acquiescence' in Article 1." Initial Report of the United States, *supra*, at para. 98.

It should be emphasized that *individual* responsibility is required. Family members of suspected torturers should not bear the consequences of a relative's actions. Similarly, mere membership in a suspect group or organization should not result in automatic responsibility for the acts of that group or organization. Defenses that preclude or limit criminal responsibility should be carefully regulated in a manner consistent with international law.[388] For example, international law restricts the availability of defenses based upon claims of superior orders or self-defense.[389] Similarly, claims of duress are also severely limited under international law.[390] Neither official immunity nor national amnesty should bar prosecution for torture.[391]

388 See generally AMNESTY INTERNATIONAL, THE INTERNATIONAL CRIMINAL COURT: MAKING THE RIGHT CHOICES (1997). The Rome Statute recognizes limited grounds for excluding criminal responsibility. See Rome Statute, *supra*, at arts. 27, 28, 31, and 33.

389 Article 2(3) of the Convention against Torture, for example, provides that superior orders may not be invoked as a justification for torture. In contrast, the Rome Statute provides that superior orders shall not relieve a person from criminal responsibility unless: (a) the person was under a legal obligation to obey the orders; (b) the person did not know that the order was unlawful; and (c) the order was not manifestly unlawful. For purposes of this article, orders to commit genocide or crimes against humanity are manifestly unlawful. Rome Statute, *supra*, at art. 33. See generally Hilaire McCoubrey, *From Nuremberg to Rome: Restoring the Defence of Superior Orders*, 50 INT'L & COMP. L.Q. 386 (2001). The Rome Statute provides that a claim of self-defense shall preclude criminal responsibility if "[t]he person acts reasonably to defend himself or herself or another person . . . against an imminent and unlawful use of force in a manner proportionate to the degree of danger to the person or the other person or property protected." Rome Statute, *supra*, at art. 31(1)(c).

390 The Rome Statute provides that a claim of duress shall preclude criminal responsibility if the duress resulted "from a threat of imminent death or of continuing or imminent serious bodily harm against that person or another person, and the person acts necessarily and reasonably to avoid this threat, provided that the person does not intend to cause a greater harm than the one sought to be avoided." *Id.* at art. 31(1)(d).

391 For a discussion of head of state immunity, see Salvatore Zappala, *Do Heads of State in Office Enjoy Immunity from Jurisdiction for International Crimes? The Ghaddafi Case Before the French Cour de Cassation*, 12 EUR. J. INT'L L. 595 (2001); Amber Fitzgerald, *The Pinochet Case: Head of State Immunity Within the United States*, 22 WHITTIER L. REV. 987 (2001); Peter Evan Bass, *Ex-Head of State Immunity: A Proposed Statutory Tool of Foreign Policy*, 99 YALE L.J. 299 (1987). For a discussion of amnesty decrees, see Human Rights Committee, General Comment 20, U.N. Doc. CCPR/C/21/Rev.1/Add. 3 (1992) ("Amnesties are generally incompatible with the duty of States to investigate such acts; to guarantee freedom from such acts within their jurisdiction; and to ensure that they do not occur in the future"). *See also* Roman Boed, *The Effect of a Domestic Amnesty on the Ability of Foreign States to Prosecute Alleged Perpetrators of Serious Human Rights Violations*, 33 CORNELL INT'L L.J. 297 (2000); Naomi Roht-Arriaza, *Combating Impunity: Some Thoughts on the Way Forward*, 59 LAW & CONTEMP. PROBS. 4 (1996).

Throughout any criminal or administrative hearings, the rights of individuals under national and international law should be fully respected. All individuals, whether in criminal or administrative proceedings, are innocent until proven guilty.[392] They should be given fair notice of any charges and a reasonable opportunity to respond.[393] In criminal proceedings, suspects should be provided with defense counsel and adequate resources to properly defend themselves.[394] When necessary, they should have access to a competent interpreter.[395] They should be notified of their right to communicate with consular officials.[396] Proceedings by a competent, independent, and impartial tribunal must be open and fully accessible.[397] Individuals cannot be compelled to testify against themselves.[398] No one should be punished on the basis of charges, testimony, or evidence that is not made available to them. Accordingly, the use of secret evidence cannot be allowed. In sum, proceedings should comply with international law and standards guaranteeing a right to a fair trial.

Direct evidence should be used whenever possible. Independent corroboration by international or non-governmental organizations should be sought. Evidence should be carefully scrutinized to determine its internal consistency and overall credibility. These rules apply with equal rigor to evidence acquired from foreign sources. Accordingly, evidence acquired in violation of international human rights norms should be inadmissible in any proceedings.[399]

392 ICCPR, *supra*, at art. 14(2)

393 *Id.* at art. 14(3)(a) and (b).

394 *Id.* at art. 14(3)(b) and (d). Pursuant to the Vienna Convention on Consular Relations, they must also be allowed to communicate with consular officials. Vienna Convention on Consular Relations, Apr. 24, 1963, art. 36, 21 U.S.T. 77.

395 ICCPR, *supra*, at art. 14(3)(f).

396 *See generally* AMNESTY INTERNATIONAL, UNITED STATES OF AMERICA: A TIME FOR ACTION— PROTECTING THE CONSULAR RIGHTS OF FOREIGN NATIONALS FACING THE DEATH PENALTY (2001). *See also* LaGrand Case (Germany v. United States of America) (Judgment) (June 27, 2001) <http://www.icj-cij.org>.

397 ICCPR, *supra*, at art. 14(1).

398 *Id.* at art. 14(3)(g).

399 *See* Robert Currie, *Human Rights and International Mutual Legal Assistance: Resolving the Tension*, 11 CRIM. L.F. 143 (2000).

In criminal or administrative proceedings, the United States should have the burden of proof in establishing that an individual has committed torture. In criminal proceedings, the government should prove its case beyond a reasonable doubt. In immigration proceedings, the government should show that there are serious reasons for considering that an individual has committed acts of torture.[400] This standard of proof is consistent with the Convention Relating to the Status of Refugees. Given the profound implications of immigration restrictions, however, this burden of proof should be interpreted to require clear and convincing evidence.[401]

Appellate review is an integral check against unfettered executive power and should be provided in all proceedings. Accordingly, efforts to preclude judicial review of either criminal or administrative proceedings should not be allowed.[402]

The rule of *non-refoulement* should be applied in cases where an individual faces the threat of torture or other cruel, inhuman or degrading treatment or punishment.[403] Indeed, the rule of *non-refoulement* should be extended to preclude extradition, deportation, or removal to a country that fails to provide basic due

400 The "serious reasons for considering" test is lower than the criminal standard of "proof beyond a reasonable doubt" but higher than probable cause. *See* Michael Bliss, *'Serious Reasons for Considering': Minimum Standards of Procedural Fairness in the Application of the Article 1F Exclusion Clauses*, 12 INT'L J. REFUGEE L. 92 (2000). *But see* ANKER, *supra*, at 423.

401 *See* Lawyers Committee for Human Rights, *Safeguarding the Rights of Refugees Under the Exclusionary Clauses: Summary Findings of the Project and a Lawyers Committee for Human Rights Perspective*, 12 INT'L J. REFUGEE L. 315, 329 (2000).

402 *See* ICCPR, *supra*, at art. 14(5).

403 Great care should be taken in determining whether there are substantial grounds for believing that an individual would be in danger of being subjected to torture. These determinations require analysis of both the particularized and generalized human rights condition in the receiving country.

> The question as to whether or not such substantial grounds exist in a given case must be assessed in the light of the particular circumstances of that case. It may be of great importance, for instance, whether it can be established that the person concerned belonged to a certain opposition group in his home country or whether he was a member of a persecuted minority group of some kind. In such matters, questions of evidence may often be difficult, and while the affirmations of the person concerned must have some credible appearance in order to be accepted, it would often be unreasonable and contrary to the spirit of the Convention to require full proof of the truthfulness of the alleged facts.
>
> In addition to the facts of the specific case, it is important also to take into account what is known about the general human rights situation in the country concerned and about the way relevant minority or opposition groups are treated in that country.

Burgers & Danelius, supra, at 127.

process rights to detained or indicted individuals, including standards guaranteeing the right to a fair trial. The current U.S. policy on *non-refoulement*, while providing some protection, also raises some concerns. In immigration cases, for example, an individual may be returned to a country if the United States receives diplomatic assurances from that country that the individual will not be tortured or if the individual is relocated to a part of the country where he or she is not likely to be tortured.[404] These exceptions should be carefully regulated to ensure they comply with the letter and spirit of the Convention against Torture and the rule of *non-refoulement*. In extradition cases, federal regulations purport to make the Secretary of State's determination of extradition, even in the context of *non-refoulement* claims, non-reviewable by the federal courts. Given the importance of *non-refoulement*, judicial review is necessary to ensure proper application of this fundamental rule.

While 18 U.S.C § 2340A authorizes the imposition of the death penalty in cases where a torture victim dies, Amnesty International USA is firmly opposed to this form of punishment.[405] The death penalty is inconsistent with fundamental human rights. Accordingly, the United States should not execute individuals convicted of torture, even when the torture victim has died. In addition, the United States should not extradite, deport, or otherwise remove an individual to a country unless the requesting country agrees to forego the imposition of the death penalty.[406]

A multi-track strategy to combat impunity

Amnesty International USA recommends the following multi-track strategy to combat impunity in the United States. While this report focuses on the United States, the multi-track strategy is one that

404 For example, relocation does not necessarily ensure avoidance of persecution. *See* ROBERTA COHEN & FRANCIS M. DENG, MASSES IN FLIGHT: THE GLOBAL CRISIS OF INTERNAL DISPLACEMENT (1998); THE FORSAKEN PEOPLE: CASE STUDIES OF THE INTERNALLY DISPLACED (Roberta Cohen & Frances M. Deng eds., 1998).

405 The original version of 18 U.S.C § 2340A did not contain a provision regarding the death penalty.

406 *See, e.g.,* Ved Nanda, *Bases for Refusing International Extradition Requests—Capital Punishment and Torture,* 23 FORDHAM INT'L L.J. 1369 (2000).

should be pursued by all countries. Indeed, a coordinated program to combat impunity through the use of domestic institutions provides an effective complement to parallel efforts at the international level.[407]

1. The United States should investigate any individual located in territory under its jurisdiction alleged to have committed acts of torture.

1.1 The Justice Department, working with federal, state, and local law enforcement officials, should investigate any individual located in territory under United States jurisdiction alleged to have committed acts of torture.[408]

1.2 The Justice Department should undertake such investigations regardless of where or when acts of torture allegedly occurred.

1.3 Investigations involving allegations of torture should be handled promptly, independently, impartially, and thoroughly by the Justice Department.

1.4 Decisions on whether to investigate and prosecute should be taken by the Justice Department, and not by the State Department or other bodies.

2. The United States should immediately take into custody or take other legal measures to ensure the presence of any individual located in territory under its jurisdiction alleged to have committed acts of torture upon being satisfied after an examination of available information that the circumstances so warrant.

2.1 The Justice Department, working with federal, state, and local law enforcement officials, should immediately take into custody or take other legal measures to ensure the presence of any individual located in territory under United States jurisdiction alleged to have committed acts of torture.[409]

---

407 These recommendations apply to all acts of torture, including attempts to commit torture as well as acts that constitute complicity or participation in torture.

408 Convention against Torture, *supra*, at art. 1(1) and 4(1).

409 *Id.* at art. 6(1).

2.2 The Justice Department should immediately take into custody or take other legal measures to ensure the presence of any individual located in territory under United States jurisdiction alleged to have committed acts of torture when issued a valid request by a foreign government or an authorized international tribunal.

2.3 No one should be accused of torture in the absence of probable cause.

2.4 Such custody or other legal measures should comply with all applicable national and international laws and standards.

2.5 Such custody or other legal measures should be continued only for such time as is necessary to enable any criminal, extradition, or surrender proceedings to be instituted.[410]

2.6 When an individual alleged to have committed acts of torture is taken into custody, the United States should assist that individual in communicating immediately with the nearest consular representative, or if he or she is a stateless person, with the representative of the state where he or she usually resides.[411]

2.7 When an individual alleged to have committed acts of torture is taken into custody, the State Department should notify the following states that the individual is in custody, the circumstances that warrant her/his detention, and whether the United States intends to exercise jurisdiction: (1) the state where the acts of torture were allegedly committed; (2) the state where the alleged offender is a national; and (3) the state where the victim is a national.[412]

2.8 When an individual alleged to have committed acts of torture is taken into custody, the Justice Department should inform the person of his or her rights, including the right to counsel and to assignment of counsel.

3. The United States should extradite any individual located in territory under its jurisdiction alleged to have committed acts of torture if it receives a valid request from a foreign

410 *Id.*
411 *Id.* at art. 6(3).
412 *Id.* at art. 6(4).

government and it ensures that the individual will not
be subject to the death penalty, torture, or other cruel,
inhuman or degrading treatment or punishment upon
extradition, unless the case is referred to the Justice
Department for the purpose of prosecution.[413]

3.1 In determining whether to extradite an individual, the
United States should ensure that the country requesting extradition is willing and able to carry out the investigation or
prosecution.[414] In order to determine willingness, the United
States should consider whether the proceedings will be conducted independently, impartially, and in a manner that
evidences a desire to bring the person concerned to justice. In
order to determine ability, the United States should consider
whether the national legal system is able to carry out proceedings consistently with international law and standards
guaranteeing the right to a fair trial.

3.2 Extradition proceedings should be conducted promptly and
in a manner consistent with international law and standards
guaranteeing the right to a fair trial.[415]

3.3 Extradition decisions should not be based upon evidence
obtained in violation of international human rights law.

3.4 All decisions on extradition should be subject to judicial
review.

**4. The United States should surrender any individual
located in territory under its jurisdiction alleged to have
committed acts of torture if it receives a valid request from
an authorized international court or tribunal.[416]**

413 *Id.* at art. 3(1) and 7(1). *See also* John Dugard and Christine Van den Wyngaert, *Reconciling Extradition with Human Rights*, 92 AM. J. INT'L L. 187 (1998).

414 *See* Rome Statute, *supra*, at art. 17.

415 Convention against Torture, *supra*, at art. 7(3).

416 The recently proposed American Servicemembers' Protection Act of 2001, which would prohibit all U.S. cooperation with the International Criminal Court, is inconsistent with U.S. obligations under international law and existing U.S. statutory provisions. American Servicemembers' Protection Act of 2001, S.857, 107 th Cong. (2001). *See* 28 U.S.C. § 1782 (federal law authorizes district courts to order a person to give testimony or provide documents for use in "a proceeding in a foreign or international tribunal, including criminal investigations conducted before formal accusation.").

4.1 Surrender proceedings should be conducted promptly and in a manner consistent with international law and standards guaranteeing the right to a fair trial.[417]

4.2 All decisions on surrender should be subject to judicial review.

5. The United States should refer the case of any individual located in territory under its jurisdiction alleged to have committed acts of torture to the Justice Department for the purpose of prosecution if extradition or surrender are unavailable or not feasible.[418]

5.1 The Justice Department should make its decision to prosecute in the same manner as in the case of any ordinary offence of a serious nature under federal law.[419]

5.2 Criminal proceedings should be conducted in a manner consistent with international law and standards guaranteeing the right to a fair trial.[420]

5.3 Evidence obtained in violation of international human rights law should not be admissible.

5.4 No official immunity or national amnesty should bar prosecution for torture.

5.5 Defenses that purport to preclude or limit criminal responsibility, such as self-defense or defense of others, should be narrowly construed in a manner consistent with international law.

5.6 Superior orders should not be a defense to torture.[421]

5.7 Duress, sometimes called compulsion or coercion, should not be a defense to torture, although it is a factor that could be

---

417 See AMNESTY INTERNATIONAL, INTERNATIONAL CRIMINAL TRIBUNALS: HANDBOOK FOR GOVERNMENT COOPERATION (1996).

418 Convention against Torture, *supra*, at art. 7(1).

419 *Id.* at art. 7(2).

420 *Id.* at art. 7(3).

421 *See Id.* at art. 2(3).

considered in certain circumstances in determining whether mitigation of punishment is appropriate.

5.8 Procedural rules, such as statutes of limitation, should not be used to bar prosecution of suspected torturers.[422]

5.9 Military commanders and government officials should be held criminally responsible for the acts of their subordinates in a manner consistent with international law.

5.10 Individuals responsible for torture should be prosecuted for their crimes, even if their actions were committed prior to 1994 (the effective date of 18 U.S.C. § 2340A).

5.11 No person who has been tried by another court for torture should be tried in the United States for the same acts unless the proceedings in the other court were not conducted independently, impartially, and in a manner consistent with international law and standards guaranteeing the right to a fair trial.[423]

5.12 The United States should provide assistance, including relocation assistance, if necessary, to victims, foreign witnesses, and their immediate families to protect them from reprisals.[424]

5.13 The standards of proof required for prosecution and conviction shall in no way be less stringent than in other criminal matters. Prosecutors must prove their case beyond a reasonable doubt.

5.14 The United States should not impose the death penalty on an individual convicted of torture. Accordingly, the United

---

422 *See* Convention on the Non-Applicability of Statutory Limitations to War Crimes and Crimes against Humanity, G.A. Res. 2391 (XXIII) (Nov. 26, 1978). *See generally* Sergio Marchisio, *The Priebke Case Before the Italian Military Tribunals: A Reaffirmation of the Principle of the Non-Applicability of Statutory Limitations to War Crimes and Crimes Against Humanity,* 1 Y.B. INT'L HUM. L. 344 (1998); Friedl Weiss, *Time Limits for the Prosecution of Crimes Against International Law,* 53 BRIT. Y.B. INT'L L. 163, 185 (1982).

423 *See* Rome Statute, *supra,* at art 20.

424 This is consistent with existing immigration provisions. For example, Congress established the S-visa category for individuals who provide valuable testimony in criminal cases. *See* 8 U.S.C. § 1101 (a)(15)(S); 8 U.S.C. § 1255. *See generally* Christina M. Ceballos, *Adjustment of Status for Alien Material Witnesses: Is It Coming Three Years Too Late?,* 54 U. MIAMI L. REV. 75 (1999).

States should amend 18 U.S.C. § 2340A to preclude punishment by death.

6. The United States should limit the scope of immigration relief available to individuals who have committed acts of torture.

6.1 Congress should adopt and the President should sign a bill revising the Immigration and Nationality Act to limit the scope of immigration relief available to individuals who have committed acts of torture.

6.2 The United States should not use immigration restrictions to circumvent its obligation to extradite or prosecute suspected torturers.[425]

6.3 Any effort to limit the scope of immigration relief available to individuals who have committed acts of torture should be carefully implemented to ensure full compliance with national and international standards on immigration relief, including the Convention Relating to the Status of Refugees.[426]

6.4 Any effort to limit the scope of immigration relief available to individuals who have committed acts of torture should comply with the inclusion before exclusion principle. Specifically, exclusion provisions should not be used to determine the admissibility of an application or claim for refugee status.

6.5 Any effort to limit the scope of immigration relief available to individuals who have committed acts of torture should require clear and convincing evidence that they have committed acts of torture.

6.6 Immigration proceedings should be conducted in a manner consistent with international law and standards guaranteeing the right to a fair trial.

---

425 See generally Jordan Paust, *Universality and the Responsibility to Enforce International Criminal Law: No U.S. Sanctuary for Alleged Nazi War Criminals*, 11 HOUSTON J. INT'L L. 337, 342 (1989).
426 While the Convention Relating to the Status of Refugees precludes refugee status to individuals who have committed egregious human rights violations, the United Nations High Commissioner for Refugees has indicated that "interpretation of these exclusion clauses must be restrictive." UNITED NATIONS HIGH COMMISSIONER FOR REFUGEES, HANDBOOK ON PROCEDURES AND CRITERIA FOR DETERMINING REFUGEE STATUS (1992).

6.7 Immigration proceedings should not be based upon evidence obtained in violation of international human rights law.

6.8 All decisions on immigration relief should be subject to judicial review.

6.9 The Immigration and Naturalization Service should not deport or otherwise remove an individual found to have committed acts of torture to a country where there are substantial grounds for believing he or she would be subjected to the death penalty, torture, or cruel, inhuman or degrading treatment or punishment.

6.10 When the Immigration and Naturalization Service deports or otherwise removes an individual found to have committed acts of torture, the United States should ensure that the receiving country agrees to investigate the case and, where appropriate, to initiate criminal proceedings.

7. The United States should establish and adequately fund an office within the Justice Department to have primary responsibility for investigating and prosecuting cases of torture and other crimes under international law.

7.1 This agency should build upon the experiences of the Office of Special Investigations, which is currently devoted exclusively to pursuing Nazi war criminals, and the National Security Unit in the Office of Field Operations, Immigration and Naturalization Service, which is currently devoted to pursuing cases of modern-day human rights abusers as well as cases of international terrorism and foreign counterintelligence.[427]

7.2 Congress and the President should allocate sufficient funding and resources to ensure effective investigations and prosecutions.[428]

---

427 Amnesty International USA takes no position on whether this federal agency should be established within the existing Office of Special Investigations, the Immigration and Naturalization Service, or some other agency.

428 For example, the Canadian government has allocated approximately $15 million per year to investigate and prosecute war crimes and related matters. In contrast, the Office of Special Investigations receives approximately $3 million per year in funding to investigate Nazi war crimes. See Canada's 2001 Annual Report, *supra*, at *passim*.

7.3 This new Justice Department office should have a highly trained and diverse staff of investigators and prosecutors. All other relevant agencies and departments of the U.S. Government should give this agency their full cooperation.

7.4 This new Justice Department office should pursue a multi-track strategy against torturers. Its primary responsibility should be to investigate and, where appropriate, extradite or prosecute persons suspected of torture.

7.5 This new Justice Department office should consult and cooperate on a regular basis with all federal agencies in its efforts.[429]

7.6 This new Justice Department office should consult and cooperate on a regular basis with non-governmental organizations in its efforts.

7.7 This new Justice Department office should issue an annual report on its activities. These reports should describe the procedures by which the agency operates in criminal and administrative proceedings. They should identify the number of individuals investigated by the agency and what action, if any, has been taken against them.

8. The United States should increase its support for civil actions filed by torture victims.

8.1 The Justice Department and the State Department should oppose the use of the political question doctrine, the act of state doctrine, or the doctrine of *forum non conveniens*, by courts in human rights cases.

8.2 Congress should adopt and the President should sign a bill amending the Torture Victim Protection Act to provide U.S. citizens with the same litigation rights provided to foreign nationals under the Alien Tort Claims Act.

8.3 Congress should adopt and the President should sign a bill amending the Foreign Sovereign Immunities Act to end a

---

429 *See, e.g.,* Executive Order 13107—Implementation of Human Rights Treaties, 34 WEEKLY COMP. PRES. DOC. 2459 (Dec. 10, 1998).

foreign state's immunity for actions alleging violations of international human rights law, including torture. This exception should not be restricted to countries designated as state sponsors of terrorism, but should apply to any state that commits or acquiesces in torture.

8.4 All federal agencies should assist litigants in human rights cases by releasing relevant documents and evidence, even if this information would otherwise be privileged under the Freedom of Information Act.[430]

8.5 The Justice Department should freeze the transfer of domestic and foreign assets of suspected torturers during the pendency of civil proceedings and assist in tracing and forfeiture of assets in the United States and abroad.

8.6 The Justice Department and the State Department should ensure that procedural rules negotiated at the international level, including agreements on jurisdiction, service of process, discovery, and enforcement of judgments, do not impede civil actions against human rights abusers.[431]

8.7 No official immunity, national amnesty, or other procedural obstacle should bar civil liability for torture.

8.8 Defenses that purport to preclude or limit responsibility, such as self-defense or defense of others, should be narrowly construed in a manner consistent with international law.

---

430 *See, e.g., U.S. Will Release Files on Crimes Under Pinochet*, NEW YORK TIMES, Dec. 2, 1998, at A3; James P. Rubin, *DPB #131*, U.S. Dep't of State Daily Press Briefing (Dec. 1, 1998). *See also* Nazi War Crimes Disclosure Act, P.L. 105-246, 112 Stat. 1859 (1998).

431 For example, the proposed Convention on Jurisdiction and Foreign Judgments in Civil and Commercial Matters, currently being drafted as a part of the Hague Conference on Private International Law, will have a significant impact on civil actions. The Convention will codify procedural rules in two areas: (1) state jurisdiction; and (2) enforcement of judgments. In its present draft form, the Convention restricts where plaintiffs may bring tort actions and where defendants may be sued. The United States must recognize the impact of these proposed rules and ensure that they do not impede the filing of civil actions against perpetrators of torture or the enforcement of legitimate judgments in foreign jurisdictions. *See generally* Beth van Schaack, *In Defense of Civil Redress: The Domestic Enforcement of Human Rights Norms in the Context of the Proposed Hague Judgments Convention*, 42 HARV. INT'L L.J. 141 (2001); Thomas E. Vanderbloemen, *Assessing the Potential Impact of the Proposed Hague Jurisdiction and Judgments Convention on Human Rights Litigation in the United States*, 50 DUKE L.J. 917 (2000).

8.9 Superior orders should not be a defense in civil actions against suspected torturers.[432]

8.10 Duress, sometimes called compulsion or coercion, should not be a defense in civil actions, although it is a factor that could be considered in certain circumstances in determining the scope of damages.

8.11 Procedural rules, such as statutes of limitation, should not be used to bar civil actions against suspected torturers.[433]

8.12 Military commanders and government officials should be held responsible in civil actions for the acts of their subordinates in a manner consistent with international law.

8.13 Congress should adopt and the President should sign legislation that would allow the federal government to file civil actions against suspected torturers when victims or their families are unable to file their own civil actions.[434]

9. The United States should increase its support, both at home and abroad, for victims of torture.

9.1 Congress should adopt and the President should sign legislation that increases funding for programs that support victims of torture, such as the United Nations Fund for the Victims of Torture. While recent legislation reflects an increase in funding from earlier efforts, it still does not adequately reflect the needs of torture victims or the programs that serve this growing population.

9.2 The United States should develop education and training programs for foreign service and immigration officers to build

---

432 *See* Convention against Torture, *supra*, at art. 2(3). Similarly, the Rome Statute recognizes limited grounds for excluding criminal responsibility. *See* Rome Statute, *supra*, at arts. 27, 28, 31, and 33. *See generally* AMNESTY INTERNATIONAL, THE INTERNATIONAL CRIMINAL COURT: MAKING THE RIGHT CHOICES (1997).

433 *See* Convention on the Non-Applicability of Statutory Limitations to War Crimes and Crimes Against Humanity, G.A. Res. 2391 (XXIII) (Nov. 26, 1978).

434 For similar legislation, see 18 U.S.C. § 229A(b).

their skills in interviewing survivors of torture and gathering evidence of these atrocities. Such efforts should build upon the experiences of the State Department's National Foreign Affairs Training Center.

9.3 The asylum claims of torture victims should be heard promptly, professionally, and with compassion, particularly where child victims or sexual torture are involved.

9.4 The Immigration and Naturalization Service should end its practice of detaining asylees, including torture victims, pending review of their asylum claims.[435]

9.5 Victims should have the right to be heard in all civil, criminal, and administrative proceedings. In these proceedings, victims should be treated with compassion, respect for their dignity, and concern for their safety.[436]

9.6 Courts should order reparations to victims, including restitution, compensation, rehabilitation, satisfaction, and guarantees of non-repetition.[437]

10. The United States should increase its support for international efforts to combat torture and impunity.

10.1 The United States should afford the greatest measure of assistance to foreign governments and international tribunals investigating claims of torture, provided that these cases are pursued in a manner consistent with

435 *See* Matthew Wilch, *Detect, Detain, Deter, Deport*, 2 REFUGEES 14 (2000).

436 *See generally* Declaration of Basic Principles of Justice for Victims of Crime and Abuse of Power, U.N. Doc. A/RES/40/34 (1985); Administration of Justice and the Human Rights of Detainees, Revised Set of Basic Principles and Guidelines on the Right to Reparation for Victims of Gross Violations of Human Rights and Humanitarian Law Prepared by Mr. Theo van Boven Pursuant to Sub-Commission Decision 1995/117, U.N. ESCOR Comm'n on Human Rights 48th Sess., Agenda Item 10, U.N. Doc. E/CN.4/Sub.2/1996/17 (1996). *See also* Michael Bachrach, *The Protection and Rights of Victims under International Criminal Law*, 34 INT'L LAW. 7 (2000).

437 *See generally* REDRESS, THE TORTURE SURVIVORS' HANDBOOK 31 (2000); Study Concerning the Right to Restitution, Compensation and Rehabilitation for Victims of Gross Violations of Human Rights and Fundamental Freedoms, U.N. Doc. E/CN.4/SUB.2/1993/8 (1993).

international law and standards guaranteeing the right to a fair trial.[438]

10.2 All federal agencies should facilitate the prompt declassification of any documents that may assist foreign investigations.[439]

10.3 The United States Senate should withdraw its reservations, understandings, and declarations to the Convention against Torture.

10.4 The United States should accept the competence of the Committee against Torture to receive and consider communications from or on behalf of individuals who claim to be victims of torture or other cruel, inhuman or degrading treatment or punishment.

10.5 The United States should support current efforts to draft an effective Optional Protocol to the Convention against Torture, which would establish a preventive system of regular, including unannounced, visits to places of detention.[440] Once adopted, the United States should promptly ratify the Optional Protocol without reservations, understandings, or declarations.

10.6 The United States should amend the federal code to ensure that acts of torture are also recognized as criminal if committed in the United States.[441]

---

438 Convention against Torture, *supra*, at art. 9. *See also* U.N. Declaration on the Principles of International Co-operation in the Detection, Arrest, Extradition and Punishment of Persons Guilty of War Crimes and Crimes against Humanity, G.A. Res. 3074 (XXVIII) (Dec. 3, 1973). Adopted by the General Assembly in 1973, this resolution requires states to cooperate in the collection of information and evidence with respect to war crimes and crimes against humanity. Moreover, states are further required to cooperate in detecting, arresting and bringing to trial persons suspected of having committed war crimes and crimes against humanity.

439 *See, e.g.*, Human Rights Information Act, H.R. 1152, 107th Cong. (2001).

440 *See* Commission on Human Rights, Report of the Working Group on the Draft Optional Protocol to the Convention against Torture and Other Cruel, Inhuman or Degrading Treatment or Punishment, U.N. Doc. E/CN.4/2000/58 (1999).

441 *See* H.R. 3158, 107th Congress, 1st Sess. (2001).

10.7 The United States should implement the recommendations of the Committee against Torture and the Special Rapporteur on Torture.[442]

10.8 The United States should ratify the Rome Statute of the International Criminal Court.

442 *See, e.g.,* Conclusions and Recommendations of the Committee against Torture: United States of America, U.N. Doc. A/55/44, paras. 175–180 (2000); Report of the Special Rapporteur, U.N. Doc. E/CN.4/2001/66 (2001).

10: Conclusion

"Torture is an assault on your most intimate and permanent identity. The struggle for that identity will continue for many years. What the torturer desires, fundamentally, is to place his voice inside your head and possess you. Your identity becomes very much embodied in the moment of torture. It makes it very difficult to get rid of."

—Ariel Dorfman[443]

Torture survivor from Chile

Despite the international consensus against torture in all its forms, the tragic reality is that it continues to occur throughout the world.[444] While countries should prohibit and punish acts of torture committed in their territory, they should also ensure that torturers from abroad do not find absolution in their territory. Torturers should not find a safe haven in any country.

The struggle against impunity is not about vengeance. It is about the pursuit of accountability, responsibility, truth, and justice. Human dignity suffers at the hands of the torturer; it suffers equally, however, in the face of impunity. The United States cannot allow torturers to escape responsibility for their actions. This is both a legal and moral obligation.

The United States has a particularly important responsibility. U.S. law and practice contributes to the development of national and international standards with respect to human rights. Throughout the world, national legislatures often look to U.S. law for guidance in drafting their own legal systems. Foreign courts also engage in such comparative analysis. Accordingly, the implications of U.S. policy on torture will extend far beyond its shores.[445]

---

443 Anne-Marie O'Connor, *Out of the Ashes*, LOS ANGELES TIMES, Oct. 22, 2000, at E1.

444 *See* JOHN CONROY, UNSPEAKABLE ACTS, ORDINARY PEOPLE: THE DYNAMICS OF TORTURE (2000).

445 *See, e.g.,* Roy Gutman, *Ruling Reflects New Global View of Justice*, NEWSDAY, Aug. 11, 2000, at A5; Bill Miller, *War Crimes Trials Find a U.S. Home*, WASH. POST, Aug. 9, 2000, at A1.

Appendix 1

Convention against Torture and Other Cruel, Inhuman or Degrading Treatment or Punishment

Adopted and opened for signature, ratification and accession by General Assembly resolution 39/46 of 10 December 1984

entry into force 26 June 1987, in accordance with article 27 (1)

The States Parties to this Convention,

Considering that, in accordance with the principles proclaimed in the Charter of the United Nations, recognition of the equal and inalienable rights of all members of the human family is the foundation of freedom, justice and peace in the world,

Recognizing that those rights derive from the inherent dignity of the human person,

Considering the obligation of States under the Charter, in particular Article 55, to promote universal respect for, and observance of, human rights and fundamental freedoms,

Having regard to article 5 of the Universal Declaration of Human Rights and article 7 of the International Covenant on Civil and Political Rights, both of which provide that no one shall be subjected to torture or to cruel, inhuman or degrading treatment or punishment,

Having regard also to the Declaration on the Protection of All Persons from Being Subjected to Torture and Other Cruel, Inhuman or Degrading Treatment or Punishment, adopted by the General Assembly on 9 December 1975,

Desiring to make more effective the struggle against torture and other cruel, inhuman or degrading treatment or punishment throughout the world,

Have agreed as follows:

Part I

Article 1

1. For the purposes of this Convention, the term "torture" means any act by which severe pain or suffering, whether physical or mental, is intentionally inflicted on a person for such purposes as obtaining from him or a third person information or a confession, punishing him for an act he or a third person has committed or is suspected of having committed, or intimidating or coercing him or a third person, or for any reason based on discrimination of any kind, when such pain or suffering is inflicted by or at the instigation of or with the consent or acquiescence of a public official or other person acting in an official capacity. It does not include pain or suffering arising only from, inherent in or incidental to lawful sanctions.

2. This article is without prejudice to any international instrument or national legislation which does or may contain provisions of wider application.

Article 2

1. Each State Party shall take effective legislative, administrative, judicial or other measures to prevent acts of torture in any territory under its jurisdiction.

2. No exceptional circumstances whatsoever, whether a state of war or a threat of war, internal political in stability or any other public emergency, may be invoked as a justification of torture.

3. An order from a superior officer or a public authority may not be invoked as a justification of torture.

Article 3

1. No State Party shall expel, return ("refouler") or extradite a person to another State where there are substantial grounds

for believing that he would be in danger of being subjected to torture.

2. For the purpose of determining whether there are such grounds, the competent authorities shall take into account all relevant considerations including, where applicable, the existence in the State concerned of a consistent pattern of gross, flagrant or mass violations of human rights.

Article 4

1. Each State Party shall ensure that all acts of torture are offences under its criminal law. The same shall apply to an attempt to commit torture and to an act by any person which constitutes complicity or participation in torture.

2. Each State Party shall make these offences punishable by appropriate penalties which take into account their grave nature.

Article 5

1. Each State Party shall take such measures as may be necessary to establish its jurisdiction over the offences referred to in article 4 in the following cases:

(a) When the offences are committed in any territory under its jurisdiction or on board a ship or aircraft registered in that State;

(b) When the alleged offender is a national of that State;

(c) When the victim is a national of that State if that State considers it appropriate.

2. Each State Party shall likewise take such measures as may be necessary to establish its jurisdiction over such offences in cases where the alleged offender is present in any territory under its jurisdiction and it does not extradite him pursuant to article 8 to any of the States mentioned in paragraph I of this article.

3. This Convention does not exclude any criminal jurisdiction exercised in accordance with internal law.

Article 6

1. Upon being satisfied, after an examination of information available to it, that the circumstances so warrant, any State Party in whose territory a person alleged to have committed any offence referred to in article 4 is present shall take him into custody or take other legal measures to ensure his presence. The custody and other legal measures shall be as provided in the law of that State but may be continued only for such time as is necessary to enable any criminal or extradition proceedings to be instituted.

2. Such State shall immediately make a preliminary inquiry into the facts.

3. Any person in custody pursuant to paragraph I of this article shall be assisted in communicating immediately with the nearest appropriate representative of the State of which he is a national, or, if he is a stateless person, with the representative of the State where he usually resides.

4. When a State, pursuant to this article, has taken a person into custody, it shall immediately notify the States referred to in article 5, paragraph 1, of the fact that such person is in custody and of the circumstances which warrant his detention. The State which makes the preliminary inquiry contemplated in paragraph 2 of this article shall promptly report its findings to the said States and shall indicate whether it intends to exercise jurisdiction.

Article 7

1. The State Party in the territory under whose jurisdiction a person alleged to have committed any offence referred to in article 4 is found shall in the cases contemplated in article 5, if it does not extradite him, submit the case to its competent authorities for the purpose of prosecution.

2. These authorities shall take their decision in the same manner as in the case of any ordinary offence of a serious nature under the law of that State. In the cases referred to in article 5, paragraph 2, the standards of evidence required for prosecution and

conviction shall in no way be less stringent than those which apply in the cases referred to in article 5, paragraph 1.

3. Any person regarding whom proceedings are brought in connection with any of the offences referred to in article 4 shall be guaranteed fair treatment at all stages of the proceedings.

Article 8

1. The offences referred to in article 4 shall be deemed to be included as extraditable offences in any extradition treaty existing between States Parties. States Parties undertake to include such offences as extraditable offences in every extradition treaty to be concluded between them.

2. If a State Party which makes extradition conditional on the existence of a treaty receives a request for extradition from another. State Party with which it has no extradition treaty, it may consider this Convention as the legal basis for extradition in respect of such offences. Extradition shall be subject to the other conditions provided by the law of the requested State.

3. States Parties which do not make extradition conditional on the existence of a treaty shall recognize such offences as extraditable offences between themselves subject to the conditions provided by the law of the requested State.

4. Such offences shall be treated, for the purpose of extradition between States Parties, as if they had been committed not only in the place in which they occurred but also in the territories of the States required to establish their jurisdiction in accordance with article 5, paragraph 1.

Article 9

1. States Parties shall afford one another the greatest measure of assistance in connection with criminal proceedings brought in respect of any of the offences referred to in article 4, including the supply of all evidence at their disposal necessary for the proceedings.

2. States Parties shall carry out their obligations under paragraph I of this article in conformity with any treaties on mutual judicial assistance that may exist between them.

Article 10

1. Each State Party shall ensure that education and information regarding the prohibition against torture are fully included in the training of law enforcement personnel, civil or military, medical personnel, public officials and other persons who may be involved in the custody, interrogation or treatment of any individual subjected to any form of arrest, detention or imprisonment.

2. Each State Party shall include this prohibition in the rules or instructions issued in regard to the duties and functions of any such person.

Article 11

Each State Party shall keep under systematic review interrogation rules, instructions, methods and practices as well as arrangements for the custody and treatment of persons subjected to any form of arrest, detention or imprisonment in any territory under its jurisdiction, with a view to preventing any cases of torture.

Article 12

Each State Party shall ensure that its competent authorities proceed to a prompt and impartial investigation, wherever there is reasonable ground to believe that an act of torture has been committed in any territory under its jurisdiction.

Article 13

Each State Party shall ensure that any individual who alleges he has been subjected to torture in any territory under its juris-diction has the right to complain to, and to have his case promptly and impartially examined by, its competent authorities. Steps shall be taken to ensure that the complainant and witnesses are protected against all ill-treatment or intimidation as a consequence of his complaint or any evidence given.

Article 14

1. Each State Party shall ensure in its legal system that the victim of an act of torture obtains redress and has an enforceable right

to fair and adequate compensation, including the means for as full rehabilitation as possible. In the event of the death of the victim as a result of an act of torture, his dependants shall be entitled to compensation.

2. Nothing in this article shall affect any right of the victim or other persons to compensation which may exist under national law.

Article 15

Each State Party shall ensure that any statement which is established to have been made as a result of torture shall not be invoked as evidence in any proceedings, except against a person accused of torture as evidence that the statement was made.

Article 16

1. Each State Party shall undertake to prevent in any territory under its jurisdiction other acts of cruel, inhuman or degrading treatment or punishment which do not amount to torture as defined in article I, when such acts are committed by or at the instigation of or with the consent or acquiescence of a public official or other person acting in an official capacity. In particular, the obligations contained in articles 10, 11, 12 and 13 shall apply with the substitution for references to torture of references to other forms of cruel, inhuman or degrading treatment or punishment.

2. The provisions of this Convention are without prejudice to the provisions of any other international instrument or national law which prohibits cruel, inhuman or degrading treatment or punishment or which relates to extradition or expulsion.

Part II

Article 17

1. There shall be established a Committee against Torture (hereinafter referred to as the Committee) which shall carry out the functions hereinafter provided. The Committee shall consist of ten experts of high moral standing and recognized competence in the

field of human rights, who shall serve in their personal capacity. The experts shall be elected by the States Parties, consideration being given to equitable geographical distribution and to the usefulness of the participation of some persons having legal experience.

2. The members of the Committee shall be elected by secret ballot from a list of persons nominated by States Parties. Each State Party may nominate one person from among its own nationals. States Parties shall bear in mind the usefulness of nominating persons who are also members of the Human Rights Committee established under the International Covenant on Civil and Political Rights and who are willing to serve on the Committee against Torture.

3. Elections of the members of the Committee shall be held at biennial meetings of States Parties convened by the Secretary-General of the United Nations. At those meetings, for which two thirds of the States Parties shall constitute a quorum, the persons elected to the Committee shall be those who obtain the largest number of votes and an absolute majority of the votes of the representatives of States Parties present and voting.

4. The initial election shall be held no later than six months after the date of the entry into force of this Convention. At least four months before the date of each election, the Secretary-General of the United Nations shall address a letter to the States Parties inviting them to submit their nominations within three months. The Secretary-General shall prepare a list in alphabetical order of all persons thus nominated, indicating the States Parties which have nominated them, and shall submit it to the States Parties.

5. The members of the Committee shall be elected for a term of four years. They shall be eligible for re-election if renominated. However, the term of five of the members elected at the first election shall expire at the end of two years; immediately after the first election the names of these five members shall be chosen by lot by the chairman of the meeting referred to in paragraph 3 of this article.

6. If a member of the Committee dies or resigns or for any other cause can no longer perform his Committee duties, the State

Party which nominated him shall appoint another expert from among its nationals to serve for the remainder of his term, subject to the approval of the majority of the States Parties. The approval shall be considered given unless half or more of the States Parties respond negatively within six weeks after having been informed by the Secretary-General of the United Nations of the proposed appointment.

7. States Parties shall be responsible for the expenses of the members of the Committee while they are in performance of Committee duties. (amendment (see General Assembly resolution 47/111 of 16 December 1992); status of ratification)

Article 18

1. The Committee shall elect its officers for a term of two years. They may be re-elected.

2. The Committee shall establish its own rules of procedure, but these rules shall provide, *inter alia*, that:

(a) Six members shall constitute a quorum;

(b) Decisions of the Committee shall be made by a majority vote of the members present.

3. The Secretary-General of the United Nations shall provide the necessary staff and facilities for the effective performance of the functions of the Committee under this Convention.

4. The Secretary-General of the United Nations shall convene the initial meeting of the Committee. After its initial meeting, the Committee shall meet at such times as shall be provided in its rules of procedure.

5. The States Parties shall be responsible for expenses incurred in connection with the holding of meetings of the States Parties and of the Committee, including reimbursement to the United Nations for any expenses, such as the cost of staff and facilities, incurred by the United Nations pursuant to paragraph 3 of this article. (amendment (see General Assembly resolution 47/111 of 16 December 1992); status of ratification)

Article 19

1. The States Parties shall submit to the Committee, through the Secretary-General of the United Nations, reports on the measures they have taken to give effect to their undertakings under this Convention, within one year after the entry into force of the Convention for the State Party concerned. Thereafter the States Parties shall submit supplementary reports every four years on any new measures taken and such other reports as the Committee may request.

2. The Secretary-General of the United Nations shall transmit the reports to all States Parties.

3. Each report shall be considered by the Committee which may make such general comments on the report as it may consider appropriate and shall forward these to the State Party concerned. That State Party may respond with any observations it chooses to the Committee.

4. The Committee may, at its discretion, decide to include any comments made by it in accordance with paragraph 3 of this article, together with the observations thereon received from the State Party concerned, in its annual report made in accordance with article 24. If so requested by the State Party concerned, the Committee may also include a copy of the report submitted under paragraph I of this article.

Article 20

1. If the Committee receives reliable information which appears to it to contain well-founded indications that torture is being systematically practised in the territory of a State Party, the Committee shall invite that State Party to co-operate in the examination of the information and to this end to submit observations with regard to the information concerned.

2. Taking into account any observations which may have been submitted by the State Party concerned, as well as any other relevant information available to it, the Committee may, if it decides that this is warranted, designate one or more of its

members to make a confidential inquiry and to report to the Committee urgently.

3. If an inquiry is made in accordance with paragraph 2 of this article, the Committee shall seek the co-operation of the State Party concerned. In agreement with that State Party, such an inquiry may include a visit to its territory.

4. After examining the findings of its member or members submitted in accordance with paragraph 2 of this article, the Commission shall transmit these findings to the State Party concerned together with any comments or suggestions which seem appropriate in view of the situation.

5. All the proceedings of the Committee referred to in paragraphs 1 to 4 of this article shall be confidential, and at all stages of the proceedings the co-operation of the State Party shall be sought. After such proceedings have been completed with regard to an inquiry made in accordance with paragraph 2, the Committee may, after consultations with the State Party concerned, decide to include a summary account of the results of the proceedings in its annual report made in accordance with article 24.

Article 21

1. A State Party to this Convention may at any time declare under this article that it recognizes the competence of the Committee to receive and consider communications to the effect that a State Party claims that another State Party is not fulfilling its obligations under this Convention. Such communications may be received and considered according to the procedures laid down in this article only if submitted by a State Party which has made a declaration recognizing in regard to itself the competence of the Committee. No communication shall be dealt with by the Committee under this article if it concerns a State Party which has not made such a declaration. Communications received under this article shall be dealt with in accordance with the following procedure;

(a) If a State Party considers that another State Party is not giving effect to the provisions of this Convention, it may, by written communication, bring the matter to the attention of that State Party. Within three months after the receipt of the communication the receiving State shall afford the State which sent the communication an explanation or any other statement in writing clarifying the matter, which should include, to the extent possible and pertinent, reference to domestic procedures and remedies taken, pending or available in the matter;

(b) If the matter is not adjusted to the satisfaction of both States Parties concerned within six months after the receipt by the receiving State of the initial communication, either State shall have the right to refer the matter to the Committee, by notice given to the Committee and to the other State;

(c) The Committee shall deal with a matter referred to it under this article only after it has ascertained that all domestic remedies have been invoked and exhausted in the matter, in conformity with the generally recognized principles of international law. This shall not be the rule where the application of the remedies is unreasonably prolonged or is unlikely to bring effective relief to the person who is the victim of the violation of this Convention;

(d) The Committee shall hold closed meetings when examining communications under this article;

(e) Subject to the provisions of subparagraph (c), the Committee shall make available its good offices to the States Parties concerned with a view to a friendly solution of the matter on the basis of respect for the obligations provided for in this Convention. For this purpose, the Committee may, when appropriate, set up an ad hoc conciliation commission;

(f) In any matter referred to it under this article, the Committee may call upon the States Parties concerned, referred to in subparagraph (b), to supply any relevant information;

(g) The States Parties concerned, referred to in subparagraph (b), shall have the right to be represented when the matter is being considered by the Committee and to make submissions orally and/or in writing;

(h) The Committee shall, within twelve months after the date of receipt of notice under subparagraph (b), submit a report:

(i) If a solution within the terms of subparagraph (e) is reached, the Committee shall confine its report to a brief statement of the facts and of the solution reached;

(ii) If a solution within the terms of subparagraph (e) is not reached, the Committee shall confine its report to a brief statement of the facts; the written submissions and record of the oral submissions made by the States Parties concerned shall be attached to the report.

In every matter, the report shall be communicated to the States Parties concerned.

2. The provisions of this article shall come into force when five States Parties to this Convention have made declarations under paragraph 1 of this article. Such declarations shall be deposited by the States Parties with the Secretary-General of the United Nations, who shall transmit copies thereof to the other States Parties. A declaration may be withdrawn at any time by notification to the Secretary-General. Such a withdrawal shall not prejudice the consideration of any matter which is the subject of a communication already transmitted under this article; no further communication by any State Party shall be received under this article after the notification of withdrawal of the declaration has been received by the Secretary-General, unless the State Party concerned has made a new declaration.

Article 22

1. A State Party to this Convention may at any time declare under this article that it recognizes the competence of the Committee to receive and consider communications from or on behalf of individuals subject to its jurisdiction who claim to be victims of a violation by a State Party of the provisions of the Convention. No communication shall be received by the Committee if it concerns a State Party which has not made such a declaration.

2. The Committee shall consider inadmissible any communication under this article which is anonymous or which it considers to be

an abuse of the right of submission of such communications or to be incompatible with the provisions of this Convention.

3. Subject to the provisions of paragraph 2, the Committee shall bring any communications submitted to it under this article to the attention of the State Party to this Convention which has made a declaration under paragraph I and is alleged to be violating any provisions of the Convention. Within six months, the receiving State shall submit to the Committee written explanations or statements clarifying the matter and the remedy, if any, that may have been taken by that State.

4. The Committee shall consider communications received under this article in the light of all information made available to it by or on behalf of the individual and by the State Party concerned.

5. The Committee shall not consider any communications from an individual under this article unless it has ascertained that:

(a) The same matter has not been, and is not being, examined under another procedure of international investigation or settlement;

(b) The individual has exhausted all available domestic remedies; this shall not be the rule where the application of the remedies is unreasonably prolonged or is unlikely to bring effective relief to the person who is the victim of the violation of this Convention.

6. The Committee shall hold closed meetings when examining communications under this article.

7. The Committee shall forward its views to the State Party concerned and to the individual.

8. The provisions of this article shall come into force when five States Parties to this Convention have made declarations under paragraph I of this article. Such declarations shall be deposited by the States Parties with the Secretary-General of the United Nations, who shall transmit copies thereof to the other States Parties. A declaration may be withdrawn at any time by notification to the Secretary-General. Such a withdrawal shall not prejudice

the consideration of any matter which is the subject of a communication already transmitted under this article; no further communication by or on behalf of an individual shall be received under this article after the notification of withdrawal of the declaration has been received by the Secretary-General, unless the State Party has made a new declaration.

Article 23

The members of the Committee and of the ad hoc conciliation commissions which may be appointed under article 21, paragraph 1 (e), shall be entitled to the facilities, privileges and immunities of experts on mission for the United Nations as laid down in the relevant sections of the Convention on the Privileges and Immunities of the United Nations.

Article 24

The Committee shall submit an annual report on its activities under this Convention to the States Parties and to the General Assembly of the United Nations.

Part III

Article 25

1. This Convention is open for signature by all States.

2. This Convention is subject to ratification. Instruments of ratification shall be deposited with the Secretary-General of the United Nations.

Article 26

This Convention is open to accession by all States. Accession shall be effected by the deposit of an instrument of accession with the Secretary-General of the United Nations.

Article 27

1. This Convention shall enter into force on the thirtieth day after the date of the deposit with the Secretary-General of the United Nations of the twentieth instrument of ratification or accession.

2. For each State ratifying this Convention or acceding to it after the deposit of the twentieth instrument of ratification or accession, the Convention shall enter into force on the thirtieth day after the date of the deposit of its own instrument of ratification or accession.

Article 28

1. Each State may, at the time of signature or ratification of this Convention or accession thereto, declare that it does not recognize the competence of the Committee provided for in article 20.

2. Any State Party having made a reservation in accordance with paragraph I of this article may, at any time, withdraw this reservation by notification to the Secretary-General of the United Nations.

Article 29

1 . Any State Party to this Convention may propose an amendment and file it with the Secretary-General of the United Nations. The Secretary-General shall thereupon communicate the proposed amendment to the States Parties with a request that they notify him whether they favour a conference of States Parties for the purpose of considering an d voting upon the proposal. In the event that within four months from the date of such communication at least one third of the States Parties favours such a conference, the Secretary-General shall convene the conference under the auspices of the United Nations. Any amendment adopted by a majority of the States Parties present and voting at the conference shall be submitted by the Secretary-General to all the States Parties for acceptance.

2. An amendment adopted in accordance with paragraph I of this article shall enter into force when two thirds of the States Parties to this Convention have notified the Secretary-General of the United Nations that they have accepted it in accordance with their respective constitutional processes.

3. When amendments enter into force, they shall be binding on those States Parties which have accepted them, other States

Parties still being bound by the provisions of this Convention and any earlier amendments which they have accepted.

Article 30

1. Any dispute between two or more States Parties concerning the interpretation or application of this Convention which cannot be settled through negotiation shall, at the request of one of them, be submitted to arbitration. If within six months from the date of the request for arbitration the Parties are unable to agree on the organization of the arbitration, any one of those Parties may refer the dispute to the International Court of Justice by request in conformity with the Statute of the Court.

2. Each State may, at the time of signature or ratification of this Convention or accession thereto, declare that it does not consider itself bound by paragraph 1 of this article. The other States Parties shall not be bound by paragraph 1 of this article with respect to any State Party having made such a reservation.

3. Any State Party having made a reservation in accordance with paragraph 2 of this article may at any time withdraw this reservation by notification to the Secretary-General of the United Nations.

Article 31

1. A State Party may denounce this Convention by written notification to the Secretary-General of the United Nations. Denunciation becomes effective one year after the date of receipt of the notification by the Secretary-General.

2. Such a denunciation shall not have the effect of releasing the State Party from its obligations under this Convention in regard to any act or omission which occurs prior to the date at which the denunciation becomes effective, nor shall denunciation prejudice in any way the continued consideration of any matter which is already under consideration by the Committee prior to the date at which the denunciation becomes effective.

3. Following the date at which the denunciation of a State Party becomes effective, the Committee shall not commence consideration of any new matter regarding that State.

Article 32

The Secretary-General of the United Nations shall inform all States Members of the United Nations and all States which have signed this Convention or acceded to it of the following:

(a) Signatures, ratifications and accessions under articles 25 and 26;

(b) The date of entry into force of this Convention under article 27 and the date of the entry into force of any amendments under article 29;

(c) Denunciations under article 31.

Article 33

1. This Convention, of which the Arabic, Chinese, English, French, Russian and Spanish texts are equally authentic, shall be deposited with the Secretary-General of the United Nations.

2. The Secretary-General of the United Nations shall transmit certified copies of this Convention to all States.

Appendix 2

Amnesty International
AI Index: IOR 53/01/99
May 1999

14 principles on the effective exercise of universal jurisdiction

"Although the reasoning varies in detail, the basic proposition common to all, save Lord Goff of Chieveley, is that torture is an international crime over which international law and the parties to the Torture Convention have given universal jurisdiction to all courts wherever the torture occurs."
—*Regina v. Bartle ex parte Pinochet*, House of Lords, 24 March 1999

Introduction

In 1945, the courts of the victorious Allies began exercising universal jurisdiction under Allied Control Council Law No. 10 on behalf of the international community over crimes against humanity and war crimes committed during the Second World War outside their own territories and against victims who were not citizens or residents. However, for half a century afterwards, only a limited number of states provided for universal jurisdiction under their national law for such crimes. No more than a handful of these states had ever exercised such jurisdiction during those 50 years, including Australia, Canada, Israel and the United Kingdom, and then only for crimes committed during the Second World War. Sadly, states failed to exercise universal jurisdiction over grave crimes under international law committed since that war ended, even though almost every single state is a party to at least four treaties giving states parties universal jurisdiction over grave crimes under international law.

The power and duty under international law to exercise universal jurisdiction. Traditionally, courts of one state would only exercise jurisdiction over persons who had committed a crime in their own territory (territorial jurisdiction). Gradually, international law has recognized that courts could exercise other forms of extraterritorial jurisdiction, such as jurisdiction over crimes committed outside the territory by the state's own nationals (active personality jurisdiction), over crimes committed against the state's essential security interests (protective principle jurisdiction) and, although this form of jurisdiction is contested by some states, over crimes committed against a state's own nationals (passive personality jurisdiction). In addition, beginning with piracy committed on the high seas, international law began to recognize that courts of a state could exercise jurisdiction on behalf of the entire international community over certain grave crimes under international law which were matters of international concern. Since such crimes threatened the entire international framework of law, any state where persons suspected of such crimes were found could bring them to justice. International law and standards now permit, and, in some cases, require states to exercise jurisdiction over persons suspected of certain grave crimes under international law, no matter where these crimes occurred, even if they took place in the territory of another state, involved suspects or victims who are not nationals of their state or posed no direct threat to the state's own particular security interests (universal jurisdiction).

Grave breaches of the Geneva Conventions. The four Geneva Conventions for the Protection of War Victims of 1949, which have been ratified by almost every single state in the world, require each state party to search for persons suspected of committing or ordering to be committed grave breaches of these Conventions, to bring them to justice in their own courts, to extradite them to states which have made out a *prima facie* case against them or to surrender them to an international criminal court. Grave breaches of those Conventions include any of the following acts committed during an international armed conflict against persons protected by the Conventions (such as shipwrecked sailors, wounded sailors or soldiers, prisoners of war and civilians): willful killing, torture or inhuman treatment, including biological experiments, willfully causing great suffering or serious injury to body or health, extensive destruction and appropriation of property not justified by military necessity and carried out unlawfully and wantonly, compelling a prisoner of war or an inhabitant of an occupied territory to serve in the forces of the hostile power, willfully depriving a prisoner of war or an inhabitant of an occupied territory of the rights of fair and regular trial, taking of hostages and unlawfully deporting or transferring or unlawfully confining an inhabitant of an occupied territory.

Genocide, crimes against humanity, extrajudicial executions, enforced disappearances and torture. It is also now widely recognized that under international customary law and general principles of law states may exercise universal jurisdiction over persons suspected of genocide, crimes against humanity, war crimes in international armed conflict other than grave breaches of the Geneva Conventions and war crimes in non-international armed conflict, extrajudicial executions, enforced disappearances and torture. Crimes against humanity are now defined in the Rome Statute of the International Criminal Court to include the following conduct when committed on a widespread or systematic basis: murder, extermination, enslavement, deportation or forcible transfer of population, imprisonment or other severe deprivation of physical liberty in violation of fundamental rules of international law, torture, rape and other sexual violence, persecution, enforced disappearance, apartheid and other inhumane acts.

It is also increasingly recognized that states not only have the power to exercise universal jurisdiction over these crimes, but also that they have the duty to do so or to extradite suspects to states willing to exercise jurisdiction. For example, the Convention against Torture and Other Cruel, Inhuman or Degrading Treatment or Punishment (Convention against Torture) adopted in 1984 requires states parties when persons suspected of torture are found in their territories to bring them to justice in their own courts or to extradite them to a state able and willing to do so.

Exercise by national courts of universal jurisdiction over post-war crimes. For many years, most states failed to give their courts such jurisdiction under national law. A number of states, most notably in Latin America, enacted legislation providing for universal jurisdiction over certain crimes under international law committed since the Second World War, including Austria, Belgium, Bolivia, Brazil, Canada, Chile, Colombia, Costa Rica, Denmark, Ecuador, El Salvador, France, Germany, Guatemala, Honduras, Mexico, Nicaragua, Norway, Panama, Peru, Spain, Switzerland, Uruguay and Venezuela. Few of these ever exercised it.

However, in the past few years, beginning with the establishment of the International Criminal Tribunals for the former Yugoslavia and Rwanda (Yugoslavia and Rwanda Tribunals) in 1993 and 1994, states have finally begun to fulfil their responsibilities under international law to enact legislation permitting their courts to exercise universal jurisdiction over grave crimes under international law and to exercise such jurisdiction. Courts in Austria, Denmark, Germany, the Netherlands, Sweden and Switzerland have exercised universal jurisdiction over grave crimes under international law committed in the former Yugoslavia. Courts in Belgium, France and Switzerland have opened criminal investigations or begun prosecutions related to genocide, crimes against humanity or war crimes committed in 1994 in Rwanda in response to Security Council Resolution 978 urging "States to arrest and detain, in accordance with their national law and relevant standards of international law, pending prosecution by the International Tribunal for Rwanda or by the appropriate national authorities, persons found within their territory against whom there is sufficient evidence that they were responsible for acts within the jurisdiction of the International Tribunal for Rwanda."

Italy and Switzerland have opened criminal investigations of torture, extrajudicial executions and enforced disappearances in Argentina in the 1970s and 1980s. Spain, as well as Belgium, France and Switzerland, have sought the extradition from the United

Kingdom of the former head of state of Chile, Augusto Pinochet, who has been indicted for such crimes. On 24 March 1999, the United Kingdom's House of Lords held that he was not immune from criminal prosecution on charges that he was responsible for torture or conspiracy to torture and the Home Secretary has permitted the courts to consider the request by Spain for his extradition on these charges.

The need for states to fill the gap in the Rome Statute by exercising universal jurisdiction. An overwhelming majority of states at the Diplomatic Conference in Rome in June and July 1998 favored giving the International Criminal Court the same universal jurisdiction over genocide, crimes against humanity and war crimes which they themselves have. However, as a result of a last-minute compromise in an attempt to persuade certain states not to oppose the Court, the Rome Statute omits such jurisdiction when the Prosecutor acts based on information from sources other than the Security Council. Article 12 limits the Court's jurisdiction to crimes committed within the territory of a state party or on its ships and aircraft and to crimes committed by the nationals of a state party, unless a non-state party makes a special declaration under that article recognizing the Court's jurisdiction over crimes within its territory, on its ships or aircraft or by its nationals. However, the Security Council, acting pursuant to Chapter VII of the United Nations (UN) Charter to maintain or restore international peace and security or in a case of aggression, may refer a situation to the Court involving crimes committed in the territory of a non-state party.

The international community must ensure that this gap in international protection is filled. National legislatures in states which have signed and ratified the Rome Statute will need to enact implementing legislation permitting the surrender of accused persons to the Court and requiring their authorities to cooperate with the Court. When enacting such legislation, they should ensure that national courts can be an effective comple-ment to the International Criminal Court, not only by defining the crimes within the Court's jurisdiction as crimes under national law consistently with definitions in the Rome Statute, but also by providing their courts with universal jurisdiction over grave crimes under international law, including genocide, crimes against humanity, war crimes, extrajudicial executions, enforced disappearances and torture. Such steps - by reinforcing an integrated system of investigation and prosecution of crimes under international law - will help reduce and, eventually, eliminate safe havens for those responsible for the worst crimes in the world.

14 principles on the effective exercise of universal jurisdiction

1. *Crimes of universal jurisdiction.* States should ensure that their national courts can exercise universal and other forms of extraterritorial jurisdiction over grave human rights violations and abuses and violations of international humanitarian law.
States should ensure that their national courts exercise universal jurisdiction on behalf of the international community over grave crimes under international law when a person suspected of such crimes is found in their territories or jurisdiction. If they do not do so, they should extradite the suspect to a state able and willing to do so or surrender the suspect to an international court with jurisdiction. When a state fails to fulfil this responsibility, other states should request the suspect's extradition and exercise universal jurisdiction.

Among the human rights violations and abuses over which national courts may exercise universal jurisdiction under international law are genocide, crimes against humanity, war crimes (whether committed in international or in non-international armed conflict), other deliberate and arbitrary killings and hostage-taking, whether these crimes were committed by state or by non-state actors, such as members of armed political groups, as well as extrajudicial executions, "disappearances" and torture.

In defining grave crimes under international law as extraterritorial crimes under their national criminal law, national legislatures should ensure that the crimes are defined in ways consistent with international law and standards, as reflected in international instruments such as the Hague Convention (IV)

Respecting the Laws and Customs of War on Land and the annexed Hague Regulations Respecting the Laws and Customs of War on Land (1907), the Nuremberg and Tokyo Charters (1945 and 1946), Allied Control Council Law No. 10 (1945), the Convention on the Prevention and Punishment of the Crime of Genocide (1948), the four Geneva Conventions for the Protection of Victims of War (1949) and their two Additional Protocols (1977), the Convention Against Torture and Other Cruel, Inhuman or Degrading Treatment or Punishment (Convention against Torture) (1984), the UN Principles on the Effective Prevention and Investigation of Extra-legal, Arbitrary and Summary Executions (1989), the UN Declaration on the Protection of All Persons from Enforced Disappearance (1992), the Draft Code of Crimes against the Peace and Security of Mankind (1996) and the Rome Statute of the International Criminal Court (1998). In defining these crimes national legislatures should also take into account the Statutes and jurisprudence of the Yugoslavia and Rwanda Tribunals.

National legislatures should ensure that under their criminal law persons will also be liable to prosecution for extraterritorial inchoate and ancillary crimes, such as conspiracy to commit genocide and attempt to commit grave crimes under international law, direct and public incitement to commit them or complicity in such crimes. National laws should also fully incorporate the rules of criminal responsibility of military commanders and civilian superiors for the conduct of their subordinates.

2. No immunity for persons in official capacity. National legislatures should ensure that their national courts can exercise jurisdiction over anyone suspected or accused of grave crimes under international law, whatever the official capacity of the suspect or accused at the time of the alleged crime or any time thereafter.
Any national law authorizing the prosecution of grave crimes under international law should apply equally to all persons irrespective of any official or former official capacity, be it head of state, head or member of government, member of parliament or other elected or governmental capacity. The Charters of the Nuremberg and Tokyo Tribunals, the Statutes of the Yugoslavia

and Rwanda Tribunals and the Rome Statute of the International Criminal Court have clearly confirmed that courts may exercise jurisdiction over persons suspected or accused of grave crimes under international law regardless of the official position or capacity at the time of the crime or later. The Nuremberg Charter provided that the official position of a person found guilty of crimes against humanity or war crimes could not be considered as a ground for mitigating the penalty.

The UN General Assembly unanimously affirmed in Resolution 95 (I) on 11 December 1946 "the principles of international law recognized in the Charter of the Nuremberg Tribunal and the judgment of the Tribunal". These principles have been applied by national, as well as international, courts, most recently in the decision by the United Kingdom's House of Lords that the former head of state of Chile, Augusto Pinochet, could be held criminally responsible by a national court for the crime under international law of torture.

3. No immunity for past crimes. National legislatures should ensure that their courts can exercise jurisdiction over grave crimes under international law no matter when they occurred.
The internationally recognized principle of *nullum crimen sine lege* (no crime without a prior law), also known as the principle of legality, is an important principle of substantive criminal law. However, genocide, crimes against humanity, war crimes and torture were considered as crimes under general principles of law recognized by the international community before they were codified. Therefore, national legislatures should ensure that by law courts have extraterritorial criminal jurisdiction over grave crimes under international law no matter when committed. As Article 15 (2) of the International Covenant on Civil and Political Rights (ICCPR) makes clear, such legislation is fully consistent with the *nullum crimen sine lege* principle. That provision states that nothing in the article prohibiting retrospective punishment "shall prejudice the trial and punishment of any person for any act or omission which, at the time when it was committed, was criminal according to the general principles of law recognized by the

community of nations". Thus, the failure of a state where the crime under international law took place to have provided at the time the conduct occurred that it was a crime under national law does not preclude that state - or any other state exercising universal jurisdiction on behalf of the international community - from prosecuting a person accused of the crime.

4. *No statutes of limitation.* National legislatures should ensure that there is no time limit on the liability to prosecution of a person responsible for grave crimes under international law.
It is now generally recognized that time limits found in many national criminal justice systems for the prosecution of ordinary crimes under national law do not apply to grave crimes under international law. Most recently, 120 states voted on 17 July 1998 to adopt the Rome Statute of the International Criminal Court, which provides in Article 29 that genocide, crimes against humanity and war crimes "shall not be subject to any statutes of limitations". Similarly, the UN Convention on the Non-Applicability of Statutory Limitations to War Crimes and Crimes Against Humanity (1968) states that these crimes are not subject to any statutes of limitation regardless when they were committed. Neither the UN Principles on the Effective Prevention and Punishment of Extra-legal, Arbitrary and Summary Executions nor the Convention against Torture contain provisions exempting states from the duty to bring to justice those responsible for such crimes through statutes of limitations.

The international community now considers that when enforced disappearances are committed on a widespread or systematic basis, they are not subject to statutes of limitations. Article 29 of the Rome Statute of the International Criminal Court provides that crimes within the Court's jurisdiction, including enforced disappearances when committed on a widespread or systematic basis, are not subject to statutes of limitation, and Article 17 of the Statute permits the Court to exercise its concurrent jurisdiction when states parties are unable or unwilling genuinely to investigate or prosecute such crimes. Thus, the majority of states have rejected as out of date that part of Article

17 (3) in the UN Declaration on the Protection of All Persons from Enforced Disappearances which appears to permit statutes of limitation for enforced disappearances. However, even to the limited extent that this provision still has any force, it requires that where statutes of limitations exist they shall be "commensurate with the extreme seriousness of the offence", and Article 17 (2) states that when there are no effective remedies available, statutes of limitations "be suspended until these remedies are re- established". Moreover, the Declaration also clearly establishes that "[a]cts constituting enforced disappearances shall be considered a *continuing offence* [emphasis added] as long as the perpetrators continue to conceal the fate and the whereabouts of persons who have disappeared and these facts remain unclarified" (Article 17(1)).

5. *Superior orders, duress and necessity should not be permissible defenses.* National legislatures should ensure that persons on trial in national courts for the commission of grave crimes under international law are only allowed to assert defenses that are consistent with international law. Superior orders, duress and necessity should not be permissible defenses.

Superior orders should not be allowed as a defense. The Nuremberg and Tokyo Charters and the Statutes of the Yugoslavia and Rwanda Tribunals all exclude superior orders as a defense. Article 33 (2) of the Rome Statute of the International Criminal Court provides that "orders to prohibit genocide or crimes against humanity are manifestly unlawful", and, therefore, superior orders are prohibited as a defense with respect to these crimes. Article 33 (1) provides that a superior order does not relieve a person of criminal responsibility unless three exceptional circumstances are present: "(a) The person was under a legal obligation to obey orders of the Government or superior in question; (b) The person did not know the order was unlawful; and (c) The order was not manifestly unlawful." Since subordinates are only required to obey lawful orders, most military subordinates receive training in humanitarian law and the conduct within the Court's jurisdiction is all manifestly unlawful, the number of situations where superior orders could be a defense in the Court to war crimes are likely to be extremely rare. In any event, this defense is limited to cases before the Court and does not affect current international law prohibiting superior orders as a defense to war crimes in national courts or other international courts.

Principle 19 of the UN Principles on the Effective Prevention and Investigation of Extra-legal, Arbitrary and Summary Executions states that "an order from a superior officer or a public authority may not be invoked as a justification for extra-legal, arbitrary or summary executions". Article 6 of the UN Principles on the Protection of All Persons from Enforced Disappearances provides: "No order or instruction of any public authority, civilian, military or other, may be invoked to justify an enforced disappearance. Any person receiving such an order or instruction shall have the right and duty not to obey it." Similarly, Article 2 (3) of the Convention against Torture states: "An order from a superior officer or a public authority may not be invoked as a justification of torture."

Duress or coercion (by another person) should also be excluded as a permissible defense. In many cases, and certainly in war crimes cases, allowing duress or coercion as a defense would enable defendants to assert the superior orders defense in disguise. In many national systems of criminal law duress or coercion is a permissible defense to ordinary crimes, if the harm supposedly inflicted by the defendant is less than the serious bodily harm he or she had to fear, had he or she withstood the duress or coercion. In cases such as genocide, crimes against humanity, extrajudicial executions, enforced disappearance and torture it is hard to conceive how committing such crimes could result in the lesser harm. However, duress or coercion can, in some cases, be considered as a mitigating circumstance when determining the appropriate sentence for such grave crimes.

No circumstances such as state of war, state of siege or any other state of public emergency should exempt persons who have committed grave crimes under international law from criminal responsibility on the ground of necessity. This principle is recognized in provisions of a number of instruments, including Article 2 (2) of the Convention against Torture, Article 7 of the UN

Declaration on the Effective Protection of All Persons from Enforced Disappearances and Article 19 of the UN Principles on the Effective Prevention and Punishment of Extra-legal, Arbitrary and Summary Executions.

6. *National laws and decisions designed to shield persons from prosecution cannot bind courts in other countries.* National legislatures should ensure that national courts are allowed to exercise jurisdiction over grave crimes under international law in cases where the suspects or accused were shielded from justice in any other national jurisdiction.
The international community as a whole has a legitimate interest in the prosecution of grave crimes under international law in order to deter the commission of such crimes in the future, to punish the commission of these crimes in the past and in order to contribute to the redress for victims. Indeed, each state has a duty to do so on behalf of the entire international community. Therefore, when one state fails to fulfil its duty to bring those responsible for such crimes to justice, other states have a responsibility to act. Just as international courts are under no obligation to respect decisions of the judicial, executive or legislative branch of government in a national jurisdiction aimed at shielding perpetrators of these crimes from justice by amnesties, sham criminal procedures or any other schemes or decisions, no national court exercising extraterritorial jurisdiction over such crimes is under an obligation to respect such steps in other jurisdictions to frustrate international justice.

Bringing perpetrators to justice who were shielded from justice in another national jurisdiction is fully consistent with the *ne bis in idem* principle (the prohibition of double jeopardy) that no one should be brought to trial or should be punished for the same crime twice in the same jurisdiction. As the Human Rights Committee, a body of experts established under the ICCPR to monitor implementation of that treaty has explained, Article 14 (7) of the ICCPR "does not guarantee *non bis in idem* with regard to the national jurisdictions of two or more States. The Committee observes that this provision prohibits double jeopardy only with regard to an offence adjudicated in a given State." (*A.P. v. Italy*, NO. 204/1986, 2 November 1987, 2 Selected Decisions of the Human Rights Committee under the Optional Protocol 67, U.N. Doc. CCPR/C/OP/2, U.N. Sales No. E.89.XIV.1). The International Law Commission, a body of experts established by the UN General Assembly to codify and progressively develop international law, has declared that "international law [does] not make it an obligation for States to recognize a criminal judgement handed down in a foreign State" and that where a national judicial system has not functioned independently or impartially or where the proceedings were designed to shield the accused from international criminal responsibility, "the international community should not be required to recognize a decision that is the result of such a serious transgression of the criminal justice process" (Report of the International Law Commission's 48th session—6 May to 26 July 1996, U.N. Doc. A/51/10, 1996, p. 67). Provisions in the Statutes of the Yugoslavia and Rwanda tribunals and the Rome Statute of the International Criminal Court which permit international courts to try persons who have been acquitted by national courts in sham proceedings or where other national decisions have shielded suspects or the accused from international justice for grave crimes under international law are, therefore, fully consistent with international law guaranteeing the right to fair trial.

7. *No political interference.* Decisions to start or stop an investigation or prosecution of grave crimes under international law should be made only by the prosecutor, subject to appropriate judicial scrutiny which does not impair the prosecutor's independence, based solely on legal considerations, without any outside interference. Decisions to start, continue or stop investigations or prosecutions should be made on the basis of independence and impartiality. As Guideline 14 of the UN Guidelines on the Role of Prosecutors makes clear, "Prosecutors shall not initiate or continue prosecution, or shall make every effort to stay proceedings, when an impartial investigation shows the charge to be unfounded." Moreover, Guidelines 13 (a) and (b) provide that decisions to initiate or continue prosecutions should be free from political, social, religious, racial, cultural, sexual or any other kind of discrimination and should be guided by international obligations of the state to bring, and to help bring, perpetrators of serious violations of human rights and international humanitarian law to justice, the interests of the international community as a whole and the interests of the victims of the alleged crimes.

8. _Grave crimes under international law must be investigated and prosecuted without waiting for complaints of victims or others with a sufficient interest._ National legislatures should ensure that national law requires national authorities exercising universal jurisdiction to investigate grave crimes under international law and, where there is sufficient admissible evidence, to prosecute, without waiting for a complaint by a victim or any other person with a sufficient interest in the case.
The duty to bring to justice on behalf of the international community those responsible for grave crimes under international law requires that states not place unnecessary obstacles in the way of a prosecution. For example, there should be no unnecessary thresholds such as a requirement that an investigation or prosecution can only start after a complaint by a victim or someone else with a sufficient interest in the case. If there is sufficient evidence to start an investigation or sufficient admissible evidence to commence a prosecution, then the investigation or prosecution should proceed. Only in an exceptional case would it ever be in the interest of justice, which includes the interests of victims, not to proceed in such circumstances.

9. _Internationally recognized guarantees for fair trials._ National legislatures should ensure that criminal procedure codes guarantee persons suspected or accused of grave crimes under international law all rights necessary to ensure that their trials will be fair and prompt in strict accordance with international law and standards for fair trials. All branches of government, including the police,

prosecutor and judges, must ensure that these rights are fully respected.

Suspects and accused must be accorded all rights to a fair and prompt trial recognized in international law and standards. These rights are recognized in provisions of a broad range of international instruments, including Articles 9, 10 and 11 of the Universal Declaration of Human Rights, Articles 9, 14 and 15 of the ICCPR, the UN Standard Minimum Rules for the Treatment of Prisoners, the UN Body of Principles for the Protection of All Persons under Any Form of Detention or Imprisonment (1988), Articles 7 and 15 of the Convention against Torture, the UN Basic Principles on the Independence of the Judiciary, the UN Guidelines on the Role of the Prosecutors and the UN Basic Principles on the Role of Lawyers. These rights are also recognized in the Rome Statute of the International Criminal Court and the Statutes and Rules of Procedure and Evidence of the Yugoslavia and Rwanda Tribunals, as well as in the Geneva Conventions and their Protocols.

When a suspect or an accused is facing trial in a foreign jurisdiction it is essential that he or she receive translation and interpretation in a language he or she fully understands and speaks in every stage of the proceedings, during questioning as a suspect and from the moment he or she is detained. The right to translation and interpretation is part of the right to prepare a defense.

Suspects and accused have the right to legal assistance of their own choice at all stages of the criminal proceedings, from the moment they are questioned as a suspect or detained. When a suspect is detained in a jurisdiction outside his or her own country, the suspect must be notified of his or her right to consular assistance, in accordance with the Vienna Convention on Consular Relations and Principle 16 (2) of the Body of Principles for the Protection of All Persons under Any Form of Detention or Imprisonment. The latter provision states that if the person is a refugee or is otherwise under the protection of an international organization, he or she must be notified of the right to communicate with the competent international organization.

To ensure that the right to be tried in one's presence, recognized in Article 14 (3) (d) of the ICCPR, is fully respected and the judgments of courts are implemented, national legislatures should ensure that legislation does not permit trials *in absentia* in cases of grave crimes under international law. Neither the Rome Statute of the International Criminal Court nor the Statutes of the Yugoslavia and Rwanda Tribunals provide for trials *in absentia*.

10. *Public trials in the presence of international monitors.* To ensure that justice is not only done but also seen to be done, intergovernmental and non-governmental organizations should be permitted by the competent national authorities to attend and monitor the trials of persons accused of grave crimes under international law.

The presence and the public reports by international monitors of the trials of persons accused of grave crimes under international law will clearly demonstrate that the fair prosecution of these crimes is of interest to the international community as a whole. The presence and reports of these monitors will also help to ensure that the prosecution of these crimes will not go unnoticed by victims, witnesses and others in the country where the crimes were committed. The presence and reports of international monitors at a public trial serves the fundamental principle of criminal law that justice must not only be done, but be seen to be done, by helping to ensure that the international community trusts and respects the integrity and fairness of the proceedings, verdicts and sentences. When trials are fair and prompt, then the presence of international monitors can assist international criminal courts in determining that there will be no need to exercise their concurrent jurisdiction over such crimes. Therefore, courts should invite intergovernmental and non-governmental organizations to observe such trials.

11. *The interests of victims, witnesses and their families must be taken into account.* National courts must protect victims, witnesses and their families. Investigation of crimes must take into account the special interests of vulnerable victims and witnesses, including women and children. Courts must award appropriate redress to victims and their families.

States must take effective security measures to protect victims, witnesses and their families from reprisals. These measures should encompass protection before, during and after the trial until that security threat ends. Since investigation and prosecution of grave crimes under international law is a responsibility of the entire international community, all states should assist each other in protecting victims and witnesses, including through relocation programs. Protection measures must not, however, prejudice the rights of suspects and accused to a fair trial, including the right to cross-examine witnesses.

Special measures are needed to deal with the particular demands of investigating, prosecuting and judging crimes involving violence against women, including rape and other forms of sexual violence. Women who have suffered such violence may be reluctant to come forward to testify. Prosecutors must ensure that investigators have expertise in a sensitive manner. Investigations must be conducted in a manner which does not cause unnecessary trauma to the victims and their families. Investigation and prosecution of crimes against children and members of other vulnerable groups also will require a special sensitivity and expertise.

Courts must award victims and their families with adequate redress. Such redress should include restitution, compensation, rehabilitation, satisfaction and guarantees of non-repetition.

12. *No death penalty or other cruel, inhuman or degrading punishment.* National legislatures should ensure that grave crimes under international law are not punishable by the death penalty or any other cruel, inhuman or degrading punishment.
Amnesty International believes that the death penalty violates the right to life guaranteed by Article 3 of the Universal Declaration of Human Rights and is the ultimate form of cruel, inhuman and degrading punishment prohibited by Article 5 of that Declaration. It should never be imposed for any crime, no matter how serious. Indeed, the Rome Statute of the International Criminal Court and the Statutes of the Yugoslavia and Rwanda Tribunals exclude this penalty for the worst crimes in the world: genocide, crimes against humanity and war crimes. National legislatures should also ensure that prison sentences are served in facilities and under conditions that meet the international standards for the protection of persons

in detention such as the UN Standard Minimum Rules for the Treatment of Prisoners and the UN Body of Principles for the Protection of All Persons under Any Form of Detention or Imprisonment. To ensure that the treatment in prison of those convicted for grave crimes under international law is in accordance with international standards on the treatment of prisoners, international monitors, as well as the consul of the convicted person's state, should be allowed regular, unrestricted and confidential access to the convicted person.

13. *International cooperation in investigation and prosecution*. States must fully cooperate with investigations and prosecutions by the competent authorities of other states exercising universal jurisdiction over grave crimes under international law.

The UN General Assembly has declared that all states must assist each other in bringing to justice those responsible for grave crimes under international law. In Resolution 3074 (XXVIII) of 3 December 1973 it adopted the Principles of International Co-operation in the Detection, Arrest, Extradition and Punishment of Persons Guilty of War Crimes and Crimes against Humanity which define the scope of these responsibilities in detail. In addition, states parties under the Convention on the Prevention and Punishment of the Crime of Genocide, the Geneva Conventions for the Protection of Victims of War and their First Additional Protocol, and the UN Convention against Torture are required to assist each other in bringing those responsible for genocide, war crimes, and torture to justice. The UN Principles on the Effective Prevention and Investigation of Extra-legal, Arbitrary and Summary Executions and the UN Declaration on the Protection of All Persons from Enforced Disappearance require states to cooperate with other states by extraditing persons accused of extrajudicial executions or enforced disappearances if they do not bring them to justice in their own courts.

National legislatures should ensure that the competent authorities are required under national law to assist the authorities of other states in investigations and prosecutions of grave crimes under international law, provided that such proceedings are in accordance with international law and standards and exclude the death penalty and other cruel, inhuman or degrading punishment. Such assistance should include the identification and location of persons, the taking of testimony and the production of evidence, the service of documents, the arrest or detention of persons and the extradition of accused persons.

14. *Effective training of judges, prosecutors, investigators and defense lawyers.* National legislatures should ensure that judges, prosecutors and investigators receive effective training in human rights law, international humanitarian law and international criminal law.
They should be trained concerning the practical implementation of relevant international instruments, state obligations deriving from these instruments and customary law, as well as the relevant jurisprudence of tribunals and courts in other national and international jurisdictions.

Judges, prosecutors, investigators and defense lawyers should also receive proper training in culturally sensitive methods of investigation and in methods of investigating and prosecuting grave crimes under international law against women, children and other persons from vulnerable groups.

Appendix 3

Response of the National Security Unit of the U.S. Immigration and Naturalization Service to questionnaire submitted by Amnesty International USA

In June 2001, Amnesty International USA sent a questionnaire to a number of offices within the U.S. Department of Justice, including the Terrorism and Violent Crimes Section, the Office of Special Investigations, and the National Security Law Division and the National Security Unit of the Immigration and Naturalization Service. The aim of the questionnaire was to clarify the role and procedures of these offices in identifying and prosecuting human rights abusers. Only the National Security Unit responded. The answers, submitted on September 6, 2001, by Walter D. Cadman, Director of the National Security Unit, are reprinted in their entirety.

U.S. Immigration and Naturalization Service National Security Unit

1. Please define the specific mandate of the National Security Unit.

The National Security Unit (NSU) is a component within the Investigations Division of the Office of Field Operations, Immigration and Naturalization Service (INS). The NSU is responsible for three areas of jurisdiction: human rights violations (with the exception of World War II Nazi matters); international terrorism; and foreign counterintelligence.

[For your information, there are very few of the latter type of case; most of the NSU's workload involves terrorism or human rights abuse—in nearly equal numbers. We also find that a number of cases are "crossover" investigations. For instance, the Front for Islamic Salvation in Algeria has been known to conduct both acts of terrorism and persecution. This is also true of individuals suspected of affiliation with the Mujahedeen-e-Khalq, an Iranian opposition terrorist organization with ties to the Iraqi regime of Saddam Hussein. Finally, it is often true of counter-intelligence cases in which the suspect was an officer or agent in a foreign government security apparatus known to engage in systematic persecution.]

The NSU establishes policy and procedure in the three specified areas, subject to approval of the INS Commissioner and executive staff. NSU monitors and, as required, directs the conduct of field enforcement operations in these areas of responsibility.

The NSU oversees INS participation in Joint Terrorism Task Force (JTTF) activities nationwide. This is significant because it is ordinarily those agents who are charged with conducting the fieldwork involving human rights abuse investigations. (This is true in both the INS and the FBI, which assigns modern day war crimes work to its International Terrorism Operations Section (ITOS) at Headquarters and to its JTTF agents in field locations.)

Working with its counterpart legal unit within the INS General Counsel's Office (the National Security Law Division, or "NSLD"), the NSU reviews all charging documents prepared by field offices in which they propose to allege violations of Immigration and Nationality Act (INA) provisions relating to persecution, terrorism or espionage. Both entities also act as the filtering units for receipt, dissemination and approval for presentation as evidence, of sensitive security information to be used in removal proceedings in any case nationwide.

The NSU routinely interacts with INS inspectors at ports of entry in its role of overseeing lookouts associated with human rights violators.

And, finally, the NSU oversees special projects with a national security nexus, such as the 1998 processing and vetting of Kosovar refugees in Macedonia and, more recently, through assignment of agents to the UN Task Force which conducted investigations into corruption and malfeasance at the refugee camps in Kenya.

2. How large is the National Security Unit in terms of staffing and funding?

Headquarters
In Fiscal Year (FY) 2001, the NSU received Congressionally approved and funded enhancements. We are currently staffing several vacancies. When fully staffed, we will maintain a Headquarters complement of approximately 25 employees: a director, a deputy director, six special agents, five immigration officers, six intelligence research analysts and several support personnel—all dedicated to our specific mandate.

An additional three NSU special agents are assigned full-time to the FBI's ITOS, where they conduct liaison on all matters of terrorism and war crimes / human rights abuse offenses. Discussions are underway for the detail of a fulltime NSU staff officer to the Department of State's Office of War Crimes Issues.

Regions
Beyond the positions mentioned immediately above, the FY 01 authorization provided funding and positions which are in the personnel hiring process, that will be used to create three regional coordinator positions—one coordinator per existing region (Eastern, Central and Western). Those coordinators will be directly responsible for acting as the bridge between headquarters NSU staff and field agents at locations Servicewide, domestically and abroad.

Domestic Field Offices
The FY 01 budget allocation provided authorization and funding for additional field INS positions to be used to augment current JTTF investigative efforts nationwide. As of October 2001, 72 INS Special Agents will represent INS at all JTTF designated cities. These agents have primary responsibility for investigating per-secutor, terrorist and foreign counterintelligence cases (there are very, very few of the latter types of case). In cities in which there is no JTTF presence, INS policy and procedure require field offices designate a primary investigative point of contact for matters involving human rights abuse or terrorism.

Overseas Field Offices

INS maintains three district offices abroad: Rome, Bangkok and Mexico City. Each of these districts, in turn, maintains numerous suboffices in various cities throughout the globe. While our overseas enforcement presence is modest, the NSU and INS's International Affairs Enforcement Branch (a separate component) are capable of deploying, and have deployed, agents to foreign sites to conduct in-theater investigations as the necessity and occasion have arisen. Such deployments are conducted, however, only upon receipt of country clearance via the United States Ambassador charged with responsibility for the location in which the agents propose to conduct their work.

3. What procedures does the NSU currently have in place in order to identify potential human rights abusers?

We recognize that no system is foolproof in today's world of unsettled conditions, record refugee flows, ready access to false identity documents, and unprecedented access to international travel. But the INS is determined that human rights abusers will not use the United States as their safe haven. To this end, in the past 3–4 years, we have developed a Servicewide set of procedures designed to focus INS' ability to detect, investigate, apprehend and prosecute human rights abusers.

As the result of the high priority INS places on human rights abuse cases, INS Field Operations issued a series of policy memoranda in 1997 and 1999, outlining standard operating procedures for the handling of 'special interest' cases, which include those in the human rights abuse category. Any case identified as involving a potential human rights abuser or persecutor is reported to the NSU. Field offices are required to notify the NSU by forwarding a report of all available information.

INS is in a unique position to use its extensive personnel resources and expertise to target human rights abusers. There are now approximately 30,000 employees within all components of the INS. Officers specializing in refugee processing, inspections, border enforcement, asylum adjudications, examinations, criminal investigations, document forensics, detention and removals, along with attorneys with expertise in immigration law, all play a significant role in targeting human rights abusers.

The NSU has sponsored yearly training conferences for INS investigators responsible for human rights abuse cases. The NSLD has done likewise. Representatives from private organizations, such as the Center for Justice and Accountability (CJA) have made presentations describing their experiences with victims of human rights abuse. These conferences reinforce the priority of these cases and ensure that agents and attorneys have the most up-to-date information available.

Domestic efforts

The INS generally encounters potential human rights abusers during the immigration process—refugee screening, initial inspection at the border, application for asylum or another benefit or during removal proceedings, and sometimes via information received from interested third parties. In many cases, human rights abusers conceal their identities and their pasts in order to acquire immigration status. If information arises indicating that such individuals have been granted immigration status through fraud, misrepresentation or otherwise illegal acts, thorough investigations are conducted.

Working with the NSU, the INS Asylum program has developed and promulgated a standard operating procedure that facilitates the early identification, detection and subsequent referral and investigation of human rights abuser cases.

But, of course, in addition to those human rights abuse cases that derive from application for a host of immigration benefits, investigations are also generated by a variety of field enforcement activities, including apprehension at a port of entry, between the ports of entry at the border, or arrest in the interior of the United States. The NSU works formally and informally with other law enforcement and intelligence agencies at the federal, state and local levels to obtain information about alleged human rights abusers who are in, or evidence an intent to come to, the United States. This communication and information exchange has facilitated our investigation and pursuit of human rights abusers. The INS and the FBI have signed a Memorandum of Understanding

(MOU) regarding the investigation and prosecution of human rights abuse crimes. The MOU promotes the effective and efficient investigation and prosecution of human rights abusers by setting out procedures to be followed and the respective responsibilities of each agency.

The INS also maintains contact with several non-governmental organizations and interested third parties that have provided lead information regarding alleged human rights abusers and persecutors in the United States.

Internationally

The NSU works closely with the INS Office of International Affairs (which has oversight of the INS Refugee and Asylum Programs and the overseas INS District offices), to ensure that aliens who have committed human rights abuses abroad do not receive immigration benefits. Screening and pre-processing of refugees is completed overseas with the objective of ensuring that protection is denied to ineligible refugee applicants who have engaged in human rights abuse or persecution. Both NSU and the NSLD continue to work with officers in the Refugee Program to develop innovative ways to screen out those who are barred by international convention and law, consistent with the generous humanitarian nature of our refugee program.

We have also engaged in unprecedented joint efforts with other governments, such as Canada, and with international tribunals. For instance, the INS has signed a Statement of Mutual Understanding with Canada that sets out policies and procedures for the exchange of information between the two countries. This sharing of information allows the INS to detect, apprehend and remove human rights abusers who may have come to the attention of the Canadian Government and then fled to the U.S. to evade apprehension in that country. We can directly attribute several cases to lead information provided by Canadian authorities.

INS is currently engaged in negotiations with the International Criminal Tribunal for the Former Yugoslavia (ICTY), with an eye toward establishing a formal MOU on the exchange of information and provision of other assistance to the tribunal in its work.

Recently, after consultations with the NSU and the NSLD, the Rwandan Government has agreed to permit INS to develop and provide training for Rwandan officers to assist them in the detection of human rights abusers.

Technological efforts
As a method to provide current information to INS field officers on human rights abuse topical and operational issues, the NSU established a NSU Bulletin Board that is accessible via the internal INS automation system. The NSU Bulletin Board lists monographs and reports on organizations that are engaged in persecution and other relevant matters consistent with the NSU mandate.

4. What channels exist for someone to bring allegations against a potential human rights abuser before the National Security Unit? How are these publicized?
The NSU has recently contracted for the production of a professional video outlining the INS role in the targeting and investigation of human rights perpetrators. When completed, we anticipate the distribution of this video to a variety of human rights organizations to increase their awareness of INS' commitment to deny human rights abusers safe haven in the United States.

We readily acknowledge that much more can and should be done to publicize federal government efforts. For example, at present no U.S. government agency—nor any of them (us) acting in concert—has undertaken anything akin to a toll-free "1-800" telephone line or the like by which complaints might be made.

5. How many cases have been referred to the National Security Unit by such external entities such as the Center for Justice and Accountability and International Educational Missions?
We cannot answer the question, because we do not categorize any cases (in the NSU or elsewhere within INS Investigations) on the basis of the source of the predicating information. There are three items we can state with certitude, though: First, we find our contacts with such entities invaluable. Second, we do receive

information of first impression from these entities and through their contacts with various refugee and migrant communities. Third, even when we receive referral from such an entity on an individual of whom we are already aware, it is helpful to be aware of the secondary referral, and to be able to "triangulate" in on other avenues of information, testimony and evidence to which we might not otherwise be privy.

6. What initially triggers an investigation into possible human rights violators by the National Security Unit?

To be exact, the National Security Unit is responsible for *coordinating* investigations into possible human rights violators, which are conducted by INS field agents located nationwide. Most of the field agents handling these cases work under the auspices of the JTTFs. When necessary, we engage the support of non-JTTF special agents to conduct investigations. And, when necessary, we dispatch agents on our own staff to supervise or, on rare occasions, even to conduct investigative activities.

Human rights abuser allegations come to our attention through a variety of sources—not the least of which is internal referral, as a suspect works his or her way through the immigration process. However, we have received leads and referrals from NGOs, other governments, international tribunals, receipt of anonymous letters, and even through admissions against interest by an individual (for a variety of reasons, the two primary being to purge the conscience of past crimes, or in the mistaken belief that admitting to affiliation with a particular group or organization guarantees a benefit grant when in fact it signals a need for further inquiry).

7. What criteria must be met before a full investigation is undertaken by the National Security Unit?

There must be reasonable grounds to believe that a violation of the administrative provisions of the INA, or of federal criminal statutes, has occurred. Often, a limited inquiry may be initiated, short of a full investigation, in order to determine whether the full investigation is warranted. Such an inquiry might be as simple as automated index checks of INS or other databases, or it could be more complex and consist of preliminary interviews with potential witnesses or cooperating sources or other, similar activity.

8. How many cases has the National Security Unit investigated?

We have not kept such statistics for a long period of time. The NSU itself only came into being in late 1997, and took on the task of human rights abuse oversight in 1998. With that in mind: to date, we have received 193 human rights abuse case referrals. I caution, though, that (a) this is a fluid number subject to daily change, and (b) the number refers *solely* to human rights abusers, not those "crossover" style cases described earlier who may have been categorized in one of the other two types of cases, but in fact also meet the statutory definition of persecutor found in the INA.

9. What percentage of these cases have resulted in the removal or exclusion of a human rights abusers from the United States?

By our count, nearly three dozen have been removed since we assumed oversight for these cases. Most of the cases described above are still within the U.S.—but, it is important to note that at least half of them have *also* been referred to an Immigration Judge and thus the expulsion process has been initiated. It is not unusual for such proceedings to last two or more years, and the issues can be incredibly complex—including adjudication of Convention Against Torture (CAT) claims made by respondents upon a finding of removability. As you are probably aware, under immigration law and regulation (and consistent with the convention), there is no bar to applicability of CAT relief, even for former persecutors.

Our experience to date is consistent with the length of many of the proceedings brought forward by the Office of Special Investigations (OSI) in Nazi cases. In the span of the 20+ years of OSI's existence, they have effected the removal of approximately 65 individuals.

In addition to the removals, though, it is important to note that INS has achieved several federal felony convictions of known human rights abusers for a variety of criminal acts, including fraud and false statements. In addition, two are pending trial.

10. How many cases does the National Security Unit currently have pending?

See the response to item 8 above.

11. What is the National Security Unit's estimate of how many alleged human rights abusers are currently residing within the United States?

We cannot say. We are aware of various estimates, some of which extrapolate from the Canadian model to arrive at a U.S. figure. Those estimates may rely, at least in part, on assumptions of parallels between the two countries' immigration and benefits systems that are not entirely comparable. What is clear, though, is the INS's responsibility to ensure that, as an agency, we work systemically and thoroughly to ensure that whenever and wherever humanly possible, human rights abusers are screened out of our benefits processes, denied entry, and expelled when found.

12. In the opinion of the National Security Unit, what steps need to be taken in order to more effectively investigate and bring human rights perpetrators to justice?

Present immigration law does not provide the INS with the necessary tools to remove individuals from the United States, even when they have allegedly committed acts considered to be atrocious human rights abuse. Currently, only three types of human rights abuse prevent someone from entering or remaining in the United States—genocide, severe violations of religious freedom and Nazi persecution. Thus, we often rely on charging alternative immigration violations against human rights abusers, and then present evidence of their persecution in the context of applications for relief from removal in the course of the hearings.

The INS has drafted comprehensive human rights abuse legislation that is currently awaiting approval of the Attorney General. It is similar to a legislative package that was provided to the last Congress, but not acted upon prior to adjournment. With concurrence of the Attorney General and the Administration, the proposed legislation will provide for additional grounds of inadmissibility and removability related to human rights abuse that will strengthen our immigration laws and enhance our efforts to pursue those individuals who do not deserve or qualify for immigration benefits.

It is also possible that existing federal criminal laws (such as the genocide and torture statutes presently found in Title 18 of the United States Code) might benefit from amending language to expand their scope.

In a non-legislative vein, we believe it is important to continue and to expand the work we have begun in the arena of establishing linkages with other partners, public and private, domestic and international, in this important work. One of the most critical, yet difficult, areas to confront is the dearth of a systematic method of information exchange among and between entities. This difficulty is often compounded, from our viewpoint, by the need to maintain case confidentiality without appearing to our partners as being uncooperative.

13. What does the National Security Unit feel should be the prime objective of the United States in holding human rights perpetrators accountable?

We are not well poised to speak for the entire government or the Administration. We strongly endorse bringing perpetrators to justice through criminal sanction, whenever possible. The first, best method of accomplishing this is in their country of nativity and citizenship—but we recognize that country conditions, or the continuing existence of certain brutal regimes often preclude this. We also recognize that some countries seek, but fail to meet U.S. judicial standards for, extradition of indicted persecutors.

Where they exist, we also strongly endorse the work of internationally constituted criminal tribunals such as the ICTY. Sometimes, though, as you are aware, this too is a cul-de-sac for lack of evidence, or because such tribunals are not adequately staffed to handle lower-level perpetrators, or large numbers of indictees.

When these mechanisms fail, then we look to prosecute within the United States—first and foremost, to determine whether a charge can be brought for the crime itself, such as torture. There are many reasons why this has not occurred to date, but it is not for lack of effort on our part. When this alternative is also foreclosed for lack of evidence, or because the crime occurred prior to enactment of the implementing U.S. statute, then we seek to investigate, arrest and charge criminally for other felony violations as I have described earlier. (Some would call this the "Al Capone" theory of law enforcement. You will recall that Capone was never convicted for murder or racketeering; he was sent to prison for income tax evasion.)

When all else fails, then our alternative is to seek removal of the individual from the U.S. under the existing administrative expulsion mechanisms found in the INA.

14. What approaches or policy choices does the National Security Unit feel can best accomplish those goals?

We have already explained our desire for amending legislation. We have described our outreach efforts, both with domestic and international investigative and law enforcement organizations. We think that both our policy and our approaches are sound, but we recognize that many of the decisions required to effect them are beyond the scope of our unit, and even of our agency. Many of these matters must be fully considered by the Administration and by the Congress before further action will occur.

15. Since the United States government has yet to seek either the prosecution or extradition for prosecution of an alleged torturer, but is making effort to deport them through sweeps like Operation Home Run, are we to understand that deportation (as opposed to prosecution or extradition for prosecution) is the primary objective of the United States government policy with regard to holding perpetrators accountable?

No, this would be an inaccurate presumption. Please refer back to our response to question number 13. It is important to state for the record that the INS, the FBI and the Justice Department all feel strongly that prosecution for torture offenses is an important arsenal in the federal toolkit. However, such a prosecution will be a case of first impression, and those charged with criminal prosecution oversight (as distinguished from investigative oversight, such as the NSU exercises) feel strongly that the initial case presentations must be strong enough to face trial, appellate and constitutional challenges. INS, working alone and in concert with the FBI, will continue our investigative efforts to their logical conclusions in each and every case that arises. We cannot, however, substitute our judgment for the prosecuting attorneys.

16. Does the National Security Unit provide regular reports? If so to whom, and what statistical information is available in those reports? If possible, please provide Amnesty International with a copy of any such reports.
The NSU has produced no past reports of the sort you mean. We have issued internal reports on human rights abusers and background information on human rights violations that are of assistance to INS field officers. Generally, reports produced by the NSU are endorsed Limited Official Use/Law Enforcement Sensitive and must be protected from unauthorized disclosure. With the granted increase in analytical staffing, we anticipate that additional reports will be developed on various organizations or regimes involved in human rights violations. You may also be interested to know that we often avail ourselves of reports issued by Amnesty International and Human Rights Watch.

We do, however, hope to produce a report of accomplishments of the type you request in the intermediate future. You may be assured of receiving a copy when completed.

Appendix 4

Resources for torture victims

ACCESS Psychosocial Rehabilitation Center
Talib Kafaji
5489 Schaefer
Dearborn, MI 48126
Phone: 313/945-8930
Fax: 313/945-8933
Email: tkafaji@accesscommunity.org

Advocates for Survivors of Torture and Trauma
Karen Hanscom
PO Box 5645
Baltimore, MD 21210
Phone: 410/467-7664
Fax: 410/467-1744
Email: klh@igc.org

Amigos de los Sobrevivientes
German Nieto-Maquehue
PO Box 50473
Eugene, OR 97405
Phone: 541/484-2450
Fax: 541/485-7293
Email: amigos@efn.org

Bellevue/NYU Program for Survivors of Torture
Allen Keller
NYU School of Medicine
c/o Division of Primary Care Internal Medicine
550 1st Ave
New York, NY 10016
Phone: 212/263-8269
Fax: 212/263-8234
Email: ask45@aol.com

Boston Center for Refugee Health & Human Rights
Lin Piwowarczyk
Boston Medical Center
Dowling 7
1 Boston Medical Center Place
Boston, MA 02118
Phone: 617/414-5082
Fax: 617/414-6855
Email: piwo@bu.edu

Catholic Social Services of Central and Northern Arizona
Mary Menacker
1610 Camelback Road
Phoenix, AZ 85015
Phone: 602/997-6105 x.3311
Email: mmenacker@diocesephoenix.org

Center for Survivors of Torture
Gerald Gray
2400 Moorpark Ave.
San Jose, CA 95128
Phone: 408/975-2750 x.250
Fax: 408/975-2745
Email: gerald.gray@aaci.org

Center for Survivors of Torture and War Trauma
Jean Abbott
1077 S Newsstead
St. Louis, MO 63110
Phone: 314/371-6500
Fax: 314/371-6510
Email: abbott4400@aol.com

Center for the Prevention and Resolution of Violence
Amy Shubitz
317 W 23rd St.
Tucson, AZ 85713
Phone: 520/628-7525
Fax: 520/295-0116
Email: ashubitz@aol.com

Cross Cultural Counseling Center
Sara Kahn
International Institute of New Jersey
880 Bergen Avenue, 5th Floor
Jersey City, NJ 07306
Phone: 201/653-3888 x12
Fax: 201/963-0252
Email: skahn@iinj.org

Doctors of the World
Maki Katoh
375 West Broadway, 4th Floor
New York, NY 10012
Phone: 212/226-9890 x230
Fax: 212/226-7026
Email: katohm@dowusa.org

F.I.R.S.T. Project, Inc.
Maria Prendes-Lintel
1550 S 70th St.
Suite 201
Lincoln, NE 68510
Phone: 402/488-6760
Fax: 402/488-6742
Email: mlintel@aol.com

Florida Center for Survivors of Torture
Faina Sakovich
407 S Arcturus
Clearwater, FL 33765
Phone: 727/298-2749 x22
Fax: 727/535-4774
Email: refugeemh@yahoo.com

Harvard Program in Refugee Trauma
Richard Mollica
22 Putnam Ave
Cambridge, MA 02139
Phone: 617/876-7879
Fax: 617/876-2360
Email: rmollica@partners.org

Institute for the Study of Psychosocial Trauma
Carlos Gonsalves
Kaiser Permanente Child Psychiatry Clinic
900 Lafayette St. #200
Santa Clara, CA 95050
Phone: 408/342-6545
Fax 408/342-6540
Email: cjgons@speakeasy.net

International Survivors Center
Westy Egmont
c/o International Institute of Boston
One Milk Street
Boston, MA 02109
Phone: 617/695-9990
Fax: 617/695-9191
Email: wegmont@iiboston.org

Jewish Family Services of Columbus
Beth Gerber
1151 College Avenue
Columbus, OH 43209
Phone: 614/231-1890 x119
Email: bgerber@jfscolumbus.org

Khmer Health Advocates
Mary Scully
29 Shadow Lane
W Hartford, CT 06110
Phone: 860/561-3345
Fax 860/561-3538
Email: mfs47@aol.com

Legal Aid Foundation of Los Angeles
Torture Survivors Legal Assistance Project #
Michael Ortiz
5228 East Whittier Boulevard
Los Angeles, CA 90022
Phone: 213/640-3921
Fax: 213/640-3911
Email: mortiz@lafla.org

Liberty Center for Survivors of Torture [#]
Fernando Chang-Muy
University of Pennsylvania School of Law
3400 Chestnut St
Philadelphia, PA 19104
Phone: 215/669-7111
Email: fchang@law.upenn.edu

Lutheran Immigration and Refugee Service [#]
Matt Wilch
700 Light St
Baltimore, MD 21230
Phone: 410/230-2721
Email: mwilch@LIRS.org

Minnesota Advocates for Human Rights [#]
Jennifer Prestholdt
310 Fourth Avenue, Suite 1000
Minneapolis, MN 55415
Phone: 612/341-3302 x11
Fax: 612/341-2971
Email: jprestyholdt@mnadvocates.org

Program for Survivors of Torture and Severe Trauma PSTT
Judy Okawa
701 W Broad St.
Suite 305
Falls Church, VA 22046
Phone: 703/533-3302 x143
Fax: 703/237-2083
Email: okawaj@aol.com

Program for Torture Victims
Michael Nutkiewicz
3655 S Grand Ave.
Suite 290
Los Angeles, CA 90007-4356
Phone: 213/747-4944 x253
Fax: 213/ 747-4662
Email: nutkiewicz@ptvla.org

Refuge
Jack Saul
NYU International Trauma Studies Program
114 East 32nd St.
Suite 505
New York, NY 10016
Phone: 212/992-9669
Fax: 212/ 995-4143
Email: jmsaul@rcn.com

Rocky Mountain Survivor Center
Paul Stein
1547 Gaylord St, #100
Denver, CO 80206
Phone: 303/321-3221 x214
Fax: 303/321-3314
Email: pstein@rmscdenver.org

Safe Horizon/Solace
Ernest Duff
74-09 37th Avenue
Room 412
Jackson Heights, NY 11372
Phone: 718/899-1233 x101
Fax: 718/457-6071
Email: eduff@safehorizon.org

Survivors International of Northern California
Margaret Kokka
447 Sutter St, #811
San Francisco, CA 94108
Phone: 415/ 765-6999
Fax: 415/765-6995
Email: survivorsi@sbcglobal.net

Survivors of Torture International
Kathi Anderson
PO Box 151240
San Diego, CA 92175
Phone: 619/278-2400
Fax 619/294-9429
Email: kanderson@notorture.org
www.notorture.org

The Center for Justice and Accountability
Sandra Coliver
588 Sutter Street, No. 433
San Francisco, CA 94102
Phone: 415/544-0444
Fax: 415/544-0456
Email: scoliver@cja.org

The Center for Survivors of Torture
Manuel Balbona
5200 Bryan Street
Dallas, TX 75206

PO Box 720663
Dallas, TX 75372-0663
Phone: 972/317-2883
Fax: 972/317-4433
Email: mbalbona@airmail.net

The Center for Victims of Torture
Douglas Johnson
717 East River Road
Minneapolis, MN 55455
Phone: 612/626-1400
Fax: 612/646-4246
Email: 104677.3412@compuserve.com

The Marjorie Kovler Center for the Treatment of Survivors of
Torture
Mary Fabri
4750 N Sheridan Road
Suite 300
Chicago, IL 60640
Phone: 773/271-6357 - Kovler
Fax: 773/271-0601
Email: mrfabri@hotmail.com

Torture Treatment Center of Oregon
Crystal Riley
OHSU
3181 S.W. Sam Jackson Park Road
UHN 88
Portland, OR 97201-3098
Phone: 503/494-6140
Fax: 503/ 494-6143
Email: rileyc@ohsu.edu

Appendix 5

Related web links

Amnesty International
www.amnesty.org

Amnesty International USA
www.amnestyusa.org

Association for the Prevention of Torture
www.apt.ch

Center for Justice & Accountability
www.cja.org

Derechos Human Rights
www.derechos.org

European Court of Human Rights
www.echr.coe.int

Human Rights Watch
www.hrw.org

Inter-American Commission on Human Rights
www.cidh.org

International Committee for the Red Cross
www.icrc.org

International Human Rights Law Group
www.hrlawgroup.org

International Rehabilitation Council for Torture Victims
www.irct.org

Lawyers Committee for Human Rights
www.lchr.org

Minnesota Advocates for Human Rights
www.mnadvocates.org

Organization of African Unity
www.oau-oua.org

Redress
www.redress.org

The Torture Abolition and Survivor's Support Network
http://torture-free-world.org/

Torture Reporting Handbook
www.essex.ac.uk/torturehandbook/index.htm

United Nations
www.un.org

United Nations High Commissioner for Human Rights
www.unhchr.ch

United Nations High Commissioner for Refugees
www.unhcr.ch

United States Department of State
www.state.gov

Witness
www.witness.org

World Organization against Torture
www.omct.org